HORSE TALES
FROM
Heaven

To Rick & Karen,
Happy Trails to you —
Sure is great doing business
with you!

Rebecca Ondov

REBECCA E. ONDOV

HARVEST HOUSE PUBLISHERS

EUGENE, OREGON

The devotions "Westward Ho!" and "Itty-Bitty Sign" were previously published in *Daily Guideposts* (New York, 2006) and are used by permission. All rights reserved.

In some cases, names have been changed in the interest of privacy.

Published in association with the Books & Such Literary Agency, 52 Mission Circle, Suite 122, PMB 170, Santa Rosa, CA 95409-5370, www.booksandsuch.biz.

Cover by Left Coast Design, Portland, Oregon

Cover photo © HuntImages / iStockphoto; backcover author photo by Deborah K. Hamilton, © 2009.

HORSE TALES FROM HEAVEN
Copyright © 2010 by Blazing Ink, Inc.
Published by Harvest House Publishers
Eugene, Oregon 97402
www.harvesthousepublishers.com

Library of Congress Cataloging-in-Publication Data

Ondov, Rebecca E.
Horse tales from heaven / Rebecca E. Ondov.
p. cm.
ISBN 978-0-7369-2758-1 (pbk.)
1. Horsemen and horsewomen—Prayers and devotions. I. Title.
BV4596.A54053 2010
242′.68—dc22
                                 2009028939

To Ray and Muriel,
my wonderful parents.
Thank you so much for making my dream of owning
my very own horse come true so many years ago.
That sorrel gelding named Andy
was the perfect Christmas gift.

By the way, remember all those prayers you said for me
when I worked from the saddle?
Good thing! In a few pages you'll find out why.

ACKNOWLEDGMENTS

To God. Thank You for never giving up on this sometimes silly girl.

To the staff of Guideposts Publications. My writing adventure began with you. You changed my life when I won your writing contest and you whisked me away, all expenses paid, to a mansion on Long Island Sound and tutored me for a week.

To Stephen Burton. You're a fabulous prayer warrior and friend extraordinaire.

To Cindy and Kim, Jeanne and Doug, Joan and Gene. How can I thank you faithful prayer warriors for standing in the gap for me? "Lord, pour out Your blessings on them."

To Julie and Michael, my sister and brother-in-law. Your enthusiasm for my writing touches my heart. Thank you for your love, kind words, and support.

To Chuck, the best brother God could have given me. I'm so glad you moved to Montana so I could join you. I love sharing adventures with you.

To Kevin. If I were to give birth to a son, I would want him to be like you. I love you.

To Bill and Dena Hooker. Thank you for being exceptional friends. Bill, you're the best backcountry boss I've ever had, and you've got the sweetest wife in the world.

To Tom Fox, my daytime boss. Thank you for "not noticing" the months I stumbled into work with bloodshot eyes from late evenings and early mornings invested in writing this book. And thank you for giving me the opportunity to work for you.

To Janet Kobobel Grant, my literary agent. Thank you for your cutting-edge leadership.

To Harvest House Publishers. It's been a pleasure working with you on this book.

To Barbara Gordon. You are an artist as well as an editor. I'm amazed at how you polished the rough edges of this manuscript yet retained my voice.

To Jack Hooker. Your ride into Cooney in '88 may have saved my life. It was a privilege to ride for you.

To all my angelic friends. Thank you for holding my hand along the path.

To the fabulous dogs that have trotted by my side, licked my face, and protected me.

To the fabulous horses and mules who were my mentors, coworkers, and companions.

Contents

A Note from Rebecca

Now I saw heaven opened, and behold, a white horse. And He who sat on him was called Faithful and True, and in righteousness He judges and makes war. His eyes were like a flame of fire, and on His head were many crowns. He had a name written that no one knew except Himself. He was clothed with a robe dipped in blood, and His name is called The Word of God. And the armies in heaven, clothed in fine linen, white and clean, followed Him on white horses (Revelation 19:11-14 NKJV).

The thought of God on a white horse *leading a heavenly army on white horses* thrills me. Someday I want to ride with them. Horses take my breath away. They are my passion. So it's natural that out of my love affair with horses I've written this collection of tales based on my experiences, most of them occurring during the 15 years I worked in the Bob Marshall Wilderness Complex in Montana. I hope you will be encouraged, entertained, and discover more about God's amazing love, grace, and provision.

1

Born Under Barbed Wire

We should behave like God's very own children,
adopted into the bosom of his family,
and calling to him "Father, Father."

ROMANS 8:15 TLB

I yawned and stretched as I slid open my second-story window. The whistle of a chickadee drifted through the still, cool air. Spring was unfolding her leaves. Next to the bubbling creek that wound through the pasture, ferns pushed aside dirt, announcing the birth of another season in the Rocky Mountains. Dawn light danced over two mares nibbling new shoots of green grass, their colts nursing at their sides.

I wiped the sleepies from my eyes. Then I squinted and frowned when I caught sight of Star, my sorrel mare, lying by the barbed-wire fence. Leaning on her front knees, she propped up her head. Her eyes were closed. Her bottom lip drooped. She looked exhausted. I leaned forward, my hands on the windowsill. Behind her on the cold, hard ground lay a large gray blob. I pressed my nose against the screen. *Oh my gosh! It's a foal, and it's still in its placental sac. And it's rolled under the fence!*

I ran downstairs, grabbed a jacket, and hustled out the back door. The door slammed as I moved toward the pasture. Star flinched. She lunged to her feet and turned around to smell the blob. Her baby was wiggling inside the sac that was halfway under the fence. The foal's head was on the far side.

My heart pounded. I'd always wanted to watch a foal be born, and this was the closest I'd come. I took a deep breath of crisp air. *Okay, Rebecca. Calm down so Star stays calm.* Casually, I strolled through the dew-drenched grass. Each tortuous step seemed to be in slow motion. I watched the blob. *Is the foal okay?* Holding my breath in anticipation, I gently ran my fingers along Star's warm coat. She nudged her foal's hind legs, issuing low nickers. I could see inside the sac. The foal struggled, grunted, and propped itself on its front knees. Its head weaved and butted the sac. It looked like a little kid with a sheet over its head. I giggled.

I slid through the fence just as the foal's sorrel head popped through. The sac folded around its shoulders like a robe. The sour and pungent smell of afterbirth gagged me. Holding my breath, I crouched down and wiped slobbery goo out of the foal's nostrils with my red bandana. Its warm breath whispered across my hands. The foal's head wobbled as it focused on me. Then it whinnied. My heart leaped. *Wow, this baby thinks I'm mom!* The barbed-wire fence squeaked as I slid between the strands, back to Star's side. When the foal put its head down, I grabbed its hind legs through the sticky sac and gently pulled it under the fence and uphill, deeper into the pasture. Star followed behind, whickering in low tones. The baby didn't seem to care the least bit about Star. Instead, it fastened its brown eyes on me and batted its long, black eyelashes.

Star licked the baby clean while I paced around it taking inventory: a filly with four heavy-boned legs; black hooves; sorrel-velveteen fur; golden, wispy mane and tail, and fuzzy, teardrop-shaped ears. *Lord, what an awesome miracle.* Star nudged the filly, who pulled her front legs under herself, pushed with her hind legs, grunted into a wheelbarrow shape, and pushed upward. She collapsed, plowing her nose into the ground.

I chuckled. The filly cocked her head to one side, watching me.

Her next attempt resembled someone trying to use stilts for the first time. She strained as she heaved herself up, straightened her legs one by one, and then propped herself upright. Suddenly one leg buckled, and she crumpled to the ground. For the next 15 minutes the little girl practiced standing…and crashing. Finally, she braced her four legs at wide angles, stood erect, looked at me, and nickered, as if saying, "Look, Mom! I did it."

My heart skipped a beat. *She's calling to me.* Love rose inside of me for this little, sticky, wet, wobbly creature. As I watched her toss her head, I thought, *Lord, does Your heart skip a beat when I speak Your name? Do you think, "Why, it's Rebecca…and she's calling to Me"?*

The filly softly butted me with her nose and wiggled her soft muzzle into my jacket. I gently rubbed the white blaze on her forehead. "Silly girl, whatcha doing?" I asked.

She gummed my jacket, tugged, and sucked. I giggled. *She's trying to nurse on me.*

Looping my arms under her belly to support her, I felt her heart beating softly. I steered her to Star's side and scooted her rear by Star's head. Pushing her side against Star's side, I tried to guide her muzzle toward the udder. But the filly stiffened her neck and stared at me. She didn't want to suckle on Star; she wanted to nurse on "Mom" (me!). I tried coaxing her, but nothing seemed to change her mind.

Lord, this isn't working. Please help, I prayed. The filly batted her long, black eyelashes at me again. Suddenly I had a brilliant idea. I tickled the filly's light-sorrel chin with my index finger. She wiggled her lips and then latched onto my finger. Guiding the filly's head with my other hand, I slowly moved my hand under Star and next to her udder. Then I did a switcheroo. I pulled out my finger and at the same time pushed a teat into the filly's mouth. It worked! She sucked, smacked her lips, and slobbered milk all over her muzzle.

During the next few days the filly gradually lost interest in me as mom, but I've never forgotten how my heart responded to her whinny. And in my mind's eye I see God's eyes twinkle when I talk with Him.

Lord, thank You for showing me that You delight in hearing my voice. Amen.

2

Westward Ho!

I know the thoughts that I think toward you, says the LORD...
thoughts of peace and not of evil,
to give you a future and a hope.

JEREMIAH 29:11

The windshield wipers scraped aside the morning sleet. Miles of red, glowing taillights lined Route 50 leading into Washington, DC. This was part of my daily routine. Each day I woke up, inched through traffic, worked eight hours, sat in more traffic, got home, walked my German shepherd named Kai, and went to bed. I was single and 22 years old. The year before I'd dropped out of college. I often prayed, *God, isn't there more to life than this?*

I grew up in a small Minnesota town but had fled the miles of cornfields by transferring to a college in the DC area. After a year in the city, I didn't know what to do with my life or where I wanted to live.

One weekend Kai and I walked along a leaf-littered trail. The breeze caressed my cheeks and the sun warmed my back. Kai bounded ahead and splashed into the creek. All he wanted was to be with me and to play outdoors. I ached for my life to be that simple. I sat on a boulder, and Kai padded over with a gift—a rock. I tossed it into the water. He dove after it, expecting adventure. *Adventure—that's what I need!* I thought. *So why am I living here?*

My dream had always been to work outside, preferably on horseback. I thought of my brother Chuck, who lived in Montana. Peace overwhelmed me when I remembered horses grazing under ponderosa pines on Rocky Mountain slopes. It was almost as if God's still, small voice was urging me to plunge into a new life.

That evening I phoned Chuck. "I'll be moving to Montana April first," I told him. "Can I crash on your floor until I get a job?"

Lord, teach me to listen to and heed Your voice. Amen.

3

The Itty-Bitty Sign

Commit your way to the LORD;
trust also in Him, and He shall bring it to pass.

PROVERBS 37:5

Slowly I drove down Higgins Avenue, moving past the brick buildings, checking off the "places to apply." I'd just moved to Missoula, Montana. Over the last week every person I'd gone to see about hiring me had said, "Try back in June when the college kids leave for the summer." I sighed. Kai nuzzled my ear. I patted him. Although my brother was gracious enough to let me stay with him, I wanted my own place, and I needed an income. I'd done everything possible to find a job.

As businesses gave way to residences, I passed a church and felt my face flush. I'd done everything...except ask God for help. *God, I'm sorry. Here I am, taking the reins again. I know You want me to have a job. Lead me. Give me a sign. And please make it obvious what You want me to do.*

Kai whined. "Okay, boy. It's time for a walk." I turned down an industrial road on the way to Blue Mountain, his favorite place to romp. On my right was a dilapidated building with a small sign that said "Saddle Shop." The little sign almost seemed to glow. I knew I had to stop.

As I opened the door to the shop, a cowbell clanked and the smell of leather greeted me. A tall, wiry man wearing a battered brown cowboy hat smoothed his salt-and-pepper beard. "Hi," he said. "I'm Snuffy. What can I do for you?"

"I'm looking for a job."

"Can you cook?" Snuffy went on to tell me he needed a cook at his ranch. In exchange, I could live in the apartment off his barn rent free. Then he gave me a lead to another job I got the next day: training 19 wild mules and 1 wild horse.

Lord, remind me to hand You the reins because You know the way. Amen.

4

Hidden

*Nothing in all creation is hidden from God's sight.
Everything is uncovered and laid bare before
the eyes of him to whom we must give account.*

HEBREWS 4:13 NIV

The alarm beeped. I reached out of my warm sleeping bag and hit the snooze button—again. My muscles ached as I rolled over and pulled the brown sleeping bag over my head. *It won't be a big deal if I sleep in a half hour. The boss isn't coming out until later this afternoon.* I'd been hired to gentle 19 mules and 1 horse. Only yesterday I'd been kicked, stomped into the mud, and run over. I was exhausted and bruised from head to toe. I reset the alarm and fell fast asleep. The next time the alarm sounded, the sun was streaming in the bunkhouse window.

I sat up in bed, stretched, and yawned. By the time I splashed water on my face and ate breakfast, the clock showed 8:30, an hour later than usual. *The boss won't notice. Besides, I needed the extra rest.* I meandered over to the tack room, pulled a couple halters with lead ropes off hooks, and slung them over my shoulder. My boots crunched on gravel as I wandered down the lane to the pasture.

The light from the rising sun glowed off the mountain peaks and a cool breeze skittered a leaf across the lane. A robin chattered as it splashed in a puddle. Glancing into the tree-studded field, I saw horses and mules on the far side. I stepped off the road and over to the fence. I put my foot on the lowest strand of barbed wire. The wire squealed as it stretched. I ducked and slid through. I hiked across the pasture, the morning dew clinging to my jeans.

When I was about 100 feet from the herd I noticed something strange. Belgium, a cream palomino draft mule, stood behind the trunk of a skinny aspen tree. He was facing me, but the tree covered his face. The rest of his body looked like an enormous balloon behind the tree. I glanced sideways. Minnesota, a lanky black mule, had his head behind a tree too. And so did Johnston, a bay mule. *They're hiding from me! They think I can't see them.* I laughed and pretended to sneak through the trees. "Hi, Belgium. I can see you. Silly boy, you can't get out of work that easy."

Suddenly I sucked in my breath. In that instant I saw myself hiding behind a tree with my body sticking out. That's what I'd done when I'd slept in late. My boss might not have found out, but I knew it was wrong. And God had been watching me the whole time. *Oh Lord, I'm so sorry. It does matter. I'll make up the time by working late.*

I eased around the tree and quickly slipped a lead rope around Belgium's neck. "You can't hide from me." I chuckled as I buckled on the halter. "And *I* can't hide from God."

I realize now, Lord, that my true character shows even when I think nobody is looking. Help me be the same person behind closed doors that I am when I know I'm being watched by others. Amen.

5

Snubbin' Post

Do not remember the former things,
nor consider the things of old.

ISAIAH 43:18

I shrugged on my jean jacket, pulled a halter and lead rope off a hook, and slipped on my black cowboy hat. The hat felt silly. Even though I'd owned a horse and ridden since I was 14, I felt like a fraud. Every day when I chummed around real, old-time cowboys I would get to thinking, *I wish I'd grown up on a ranch. If I'd grown up punching cows, I would've earned the right to wear a cowboy hat.* My boss insisted that his crew wear cowboy hats on the pack trips we guided, but until then… I hung the hat on its peg, opened the door, stepped onto the porch, and closed the door behind me.

The spring clouds hung low on the mountains, trapping a cold mist in the air. I headed to the corral, slogging through deep mud. With each step the gooey mess threatened to suck the boots off my feet. Today I was going to catch the new chocolate-brown gelding. He'd been dubbed Dusty because he wasn't much to look at. The horse was a middle-aged, snorty critter stuck in with the wild mules and horse

I was working with. I unbuckled the halter and slipped it over my shoulder, attempting to hide it. *Too late!* The horses and mules saw the halter, snorted, and galloped to the other side of the pasture. *Not again,* I moaned. This was the hardest part of the job—separating one of the wild-eyed buggers from the herd in a 10-acre field. *If I'd grown up on a ranch, I would have learned to rope,* I groused.

I chased after the herd, trying to keep my boots on by curling my toes. I huffed and puffed as I zigzagged, cutting out the extra animals and keeping Dusty in the center of my vision. Finally the now smaller group stampeded into a corner of the field. Sweat rolled down my back. My side hurt from running. I gave the critters plenty of room to mill around while I stood panting. One by one I let the other horse and mules spurt out, until only Dusty stood in the corner, snorting and blowing. His eyes brimmed with fear. I looked at the ground, lowered my voice, and spoke slowly, "That a boy. You must have had something pretty bad happen to you to make you this scared."

Dusty's eyes looked left and then right. He bolted. I sprinted and blocked him. "You're not going anywhere without this halter on," I told him. For the next half hour I stepped forward until he squirmed, and then backed up one step to give him room to breathe. Forward and back we went as he got used to me. Soon he let me rub his neck with the rope, which I gently put around his neck. I pulled on the halter and buckled it up. I turned around and headed toward the corrals, and Dusty followed me like he'd been handled quite a bit. I led him out of the pasture, tied him to the snubbing post next to the tack shed, and brushed him down. He goosed a little, but I found some of his itchy spots. Pretty soon he leaned into the brush and relaxed.

Suddenly he jumped straight into the air. He came down snorting and blowing, the whites of his eyes showing.

I quickly stepped back and glanced around to see what spooked him. I didn't see anything unusual. *Somebody must have really hurt this horse,* I repeated.

Dusty was sure he'd seen a bogeyman. He bucked, hauled back, and hit the end of the lead rope. He jumped forward, slamming into the post. It cracked. He hauled back again, this time digging in with his hind legs. He whipped his head back and forth with all his might. Crack! The snubbing post snapped and jerked into Dusty's chest. The horse swung around. Because the lead rope held fast to the halter and the post, the post end slammed into Dusty's hindquarters.

He jumped, causing the lead rope to snap the post toward him again. It hit hard, and Dusty bolted down the driveway as if he were on the last turn at the Kentucky Derby. I stood in a cloud of dust watching the broken post chase him out of sight.

God, protect him, I quickly prayed as I dashed over and fired up the pickup. Taking off I followed that cloud. *What if he breaks a leg? Or falls off a cliff?* Three miles later the road wound between towering limestone cliffs. I rounded the bend. There he stood. White lather blanketed him from head to hoof. I frowned. Dusty looked like a different horse. He calmly stood and munched grass in a ditch. Next to him was the remnant of post, still securely tied to the lead rope.

Dusty had spooked because of being abused in his past. The harder he ran from it, the harder the post beat him. When he quit running, he learned that the post quit whacking him. So, basically, instead of running from his past, Dusty used it as a starting place. From that time on, Dusty was the calmest, most levelheaded guest horse on the ranch. After that day, nothing spooked him.

The next morning I took Dusty's lesson to heart. I quit tying my past to a snubbin' post and, instead, used it as a starting place. I slipped on my cowboy hat and headed to the corral. I hadn't been raised on a ranch, but I earned my hat each day I slogged through the mud chasing critters and every night when I took in Western lore by peppering my old-time cowboy friends with questions. They gave me the leg up I would need to ride into the wilderness.

Lord, thanks for teaching me to use my past as a tool to build my future. Amen.

6

Sling Rope

*It is absolutely clear that God has called you to a free life.
Just make sure that you don't use this freedom as
an excuse to do whatever you want to do and
destroy your freedom. Rather, use your freedom to
serve one another in love; that's how freedom grows.*

GALATIANS 5:13 MSG

The pines gently swayed in the warm afternoon breeze. Minnesota, a black mule with a white nose, stood tied to the hitching rack next to the barn. The last couple months I'd been gentling mules and a horse that were pastured by Snuffy's place. He was the saddle maker who'd hired me as a cook and told me about the ranching job. With a blue plastic curry comb I brushed clumps of dirt off Minnesota's back and then shook the brush at him. "I'll bet you don't realize it yet, but you're getting saddled again today." I lowered the brush. "Only I wish I knew how to slap a load on the saddle. Snuffy was supposed to be here." I swept the curry comb across his sides in tight circles. Minnesota leaned into the brush as he basked in the attention. Normally brushing the mules was as relaxing for me as it was for them, but today I was troubled. I kept rewinding the conversation I'd had with Gail last night.

I'd met Gail shortly after I moved to Missoula. I hadn't made many friends yet, so it was fun to hang out in town together. She seemed like a go-getter because she always talked about her future. Then last night she phoned and invited me over to her mom's to spend the evening doing "star charts." I hadn't heard of them, so I asked what they were. She excitedly replied, "Mom and I can help you map out your future! Using charts that show the movement of the stars, we can foretell what's going to happen. And it really works too."

I wound the phone cord around my little finger. "So is this like fortune-telling?"

"No, this is more exact because we use star charts."

"I'll pass."

Gail's voice became forceful and defensive. "There isn't anything wrong with it. It's all scientific."

I squirmed in the wooden captain's chair.

Gail's voice grew hard. "What's wrong with just seeing what the charts say? Are you a prude or something?"

I chewed on my lip. "No thanks," I replied. Even as I hung up the phone her words were stabbing me. *Was I a prude? Did my beliefs bind me?*

I brushed one last clump of dirt off Minnesota's neck. I walked into the barn and pulled a packsaddle and saddle pad off a rack. Stepping next to the mule, I flipped the saddle pad on his back. As I swung the saddle in place, Snuffy roared down the driveway in his green pickup. He pulled up next to the hitching rack. Unfolding his tall, wiry frame from the truck, he slipped on his brown cowboy hat. "Got hung up at the shop, but it looks like I made it in time. Let's load that mule."

I smiled, very relieved. "That'd be great." I buckled the saddle straps and tightened the cinch while Snuffy "mantied" a couple bales of hay—wrapping and tying them in two heavy-duty canvas tarps. He lugged them over to Minnesota and placed them on the ground, one on each side of the mule. He reached up on the saddle and tugged on a bundle of rope that was neatly looped through one of the saddle's D rings. "This is called a sling rope," he instructed.

"I know that." I giggled. "But I don't have a clue how to use it."

Snuffy loosened the rope. "See how this end is tied to the front D ring? Then we slide the rope through the back D ring and let the loose end hang down," he said, demonstrating. "Now I'm pulling the middle of the rope down to form a loop supported by the front and back D rings." The loop was so big that it hung down to Minnesota's knees. Snuffy stroked his salt-and-pepper-colored beard and looked at me. "Stand back while I load the hay. There's no telling what this mule's going to think of these packs and their weight."

I stepped back 10 feet.

The cowboy rubbed Minnesota's shoulder. "Now you just mind your business," Snuffy said soothingly. He turned and placed his feet next to the first pack. He lifted the closest end of the 80-pound canvas-wrapped hay bale to his knees and reached out and grabbed the other end. In one swift motion he hefted the pack up so it rested on his knees, swiveled, and heaved it up against the pack saddle, leaning his chest against the bottom to support it.

Minnesota nonchalantly looked back at the pack.

Snuffy pulled the sling rope that hung loose from the back D ring and adjusted the loop so it tightened across the top third of the load. Across the middle of the load he threaded the end of the rope through the now-snug loop, forming a smaller loop. Now he tugged harder on the rope next to the back D ring. "Watch how the sling rope sucks the pack into the D rings." Wiggling the pack with his shoulder while push-ing it hard against the saddle, he pulled until the loop around the load was tight. "I made the smaller loop earlier because the rope is so tight now I'd never be able to thread the rope through to tie off." He grabbed the rope's loose end and pulled it taut across the bottom of the pack and up to the upper loop, where he tied it off with a quick knot.

He moved to the other side of Minnesota and did the same thing with the second sling rope and pack. He stood back and scratched the critter's neck. "You're a good mule. You act like you've been loaded every day of your life." Minnesota closed his eyes and leaned into the Snuffy's rubbing.

The cowboy placed his hand on the top of the pack. "This is the really cool thing about a sling rope." Sharply he pulled down, making the packs rock from side to side. "The packs rock like this when the mule walks. If you place the sling rope around the pack at just the right spot, it holds the packs in balance." Once again he rocked the packs. "Oftentimes the bottom of the pack bangs against a rock, or the side of a cliff, or even a tree." He pushed the bottom of the pack toward Minnesota's rear, tipping it off kilter. As the saddle rocked, the sling rope allowed the pack to straighten itself. "Did you see how the sling rope didn't bind the load? Instead, it offered support by giving the load freedom to adjust back to the balanced position."

Once again he pushed the bottom of the pack off kilter. While I watched it rock, his words seeped into me. *Bind...the sling rope doesn't bind. Instead it supports. That's what my beliefs were doing. They weren't binding me. They were supporting me by keeping me free from sin and in balance with God. Sin is bondage. Gail has it twisted backward.*

As the pack righted itself and quit rocking, relief flooded through me. Maybe I am a prude for God, but I want to be. And I'm not going to feel bad or apologize.

> *Thank You, Lord, for giving me Your Word to support me and keep me free from sin. Help me be courageous and stand strong in my relationship with You. Amen.*

7

Bob Marshall

Where there is no vision, the people perish.

PROVERBS 29:18 KJV

The spring breeze drifted over the snowy peaks and carried a bone-chilling cold down the mountains. The rocky ledge next to the trail skirted the sheer mountainside. Larry, the boss, rode his bay Arabian gelding in the lead. Single file behind him rode the guests, with me bringing up the rear. Straining their hindquarters, the horses clambered up the steep trail, their hooves clattering across the rocks. In a few minutes we'd be at the top of Limestone Pass. I buttoned my prickly wool jacket and centered my weight in the saddle. Nervously I patted Sunrise's neck. The trail was only a few feet wide. I glanced to my left. The mountain rose so steeply I could almost reach out and touch the yellow arnica flowers growing in the cliff. My right stirrup hung over nothingness. The edge of the trail dropped off into a steep gully.

Julie, the guest who rode in front of me, grabbed her tan cowboy hat as the breeze tugged at it. She tightened the stampede strap. I watched her glance down the cliff, where her hat would have blown had it gotten away. Then she riveted her eyes on the horse in front of her. Trying to make conversation to overcome her nervousness, she shouted over the breeze, "Rebecca, how long have you been doing this?"

I cringed and shouted back, "Not long enough." The wind stole my words, and I was glad. I didn't want to tell her that this was my first season working as a cook on a pack trip. I felt so inadequate. This was something I'd dreamed of doing, but I didn't have any experience. I'd been raised on the flat prairies of Minnesota. Before this summer I'd never ridden a horse in mountains. I was just as nervous about this cliff as Julie was. Other than a couple short canoe trips and backpack excursions, I hadn't spent any time in the wilderness. And cooking? As a kid I'd whipped up a couple meals for my family on an electric range. I looked down at the narrow trail. *How did I land this job?*

The horses scrambled up the last steep section of the trail and onto the flat ground of the pass. We wound through a green meadow of tall grass and skirted a muddy elk wallow. The wind blasted us as we rode through the corridor between knobby mountaintops. Rounding a bend, the trail view opened up to reveal a stunning panoramic vista. Rows of snow-capped mountain peaks studded the horizon for miles. I stared in awe at the raw beauty.

Larry reined his horse up a small incline and stopped next to a brown U.S. Forest Service sign that stood in a pile of rocks a few feet off the trail. The guests and I rode over and formed a semicircle around him.

Larry zipped up his brown vest and pulled down his dusty cowboy hat. Pointing to the sign that read "Bob Marshall Wilderness," he shouted above the howl of the wind, "Does anybody know who Bob Marshall was?"

The guests looked at each other and shrugged. I ducked my head, hoping he wouldn't call on me.

Larry rubbed his brown beard and grinned. "Bob was born in the early twentieth century in Manhattan to a wealthy, socially elite family." Larry went on to explain that instead of pursuing wealth, Bob was fascinated with tales of Lewis and Clark's expedition. This spurred him to tackle a trek through the Adirondack Mountains. And hike he did. He went on to climb all 46 peaks in that region. After graduating from college with a forestry degree, he invested every moment of time climbing peaks and exploring the backwoods. He became famous for his 40- to 50-mile per day hikes.

Larry's horse impatiently stomped its foot.

My saddle creaked as I shifted my weight. *I can't imagine hiking 12 miles a day in the mountains, much less 40!*

Larry leaned forward, resting his arm on the saddle horn. He shared about Bob's love for nature, which became a passion to create protected wilderness areas for people to enjoy. He could see the writing on the wall—that in a few short years corporate America would dig ore mines, clear-cut trees, and drill oil wells everywhere they could. He wanted to protect the land by making it public and passing regulations for its use—a very innovative idea at that time. He didn't know if it could be done, but he would fight for his vision.

Larry's horse bobbed its head. He gathered the reins and continued talking. "Against heavy opposition, he is credited with singlehandedly getting more than 5.4 million acres set aside as national wilderness areas."

I shook my head. *Wow, that's a lot of land.*

Larry turned his horse away from the group and faced the panoramic view. "He died at the age of 38, and this wilderness area was set aside in honor of him." Larry swept his gloved hand over the peaks. "This area is called the crown jewel of the American wilderness system. The 'Bob Marshall Complex' takes in over 1.5 million acres, nearly double the size of the state of Rhode Island. And there's not one road through it."

I looked at the crystalline-blue sky with rows of snow-capped peaks stretching the horizon. A grand view. A momentous monument to the grand victory won by a man with a passion. A man doing something unprecedented. I shuddered. I'd been ashamed to admit that I was a greenhorn when it came to cooking and pack trips, but when Bob

Marshall began, he wasn't qualified either. He became knowledgeable throughout his life journey. The huge national wilderness system had started with one man's passion. As Bob gained confidence, he reached forward by setting new goals.

I straightened in the saddle. *That's what I need to do.* I'd felt inadequate because I had reached my goal of working in the woods, but I was overwhelmed by all the things I didn't know and needed to learn. The problem was that I'd failed to set my next goal. *I want to be an accomplished outdoorswoman. Most of all, I want to help people enjoy their pack trips in the back country. But where do I start?* I gazed at the peaks. My palomino horse impatiently stomped her foot. I looked down at her hoof. A still, small voice seemed to whisper in my spirit, saying, "Start here. At this spot, where you are right now." I grinned. *How simple is that?* I rested my arms on the saddle horn and leaned forward while my mind cataloged the details about Bob Marshall. *That's great information to share with future guests.*

Over the next couple of years I focused on soaking up every tidbit I came across about living in the woods and helping people get the most out of their time in the mountains. The more I learned, the more confident I became. The more confident I became, the steeper I set my new goals.

> *Lord, help me set goals so I will grow spiritually strong and have the confidence to pursue the dreams You've placed within my heart. Amen.*

8

Mudslide Mule

*For the waywardness of the simple will kill them,
and the complacency of fools will destroy them;
but whoever listens to me will live in safety
and be at ease, without fear of harm.*

PROVERBS 1:32-33 NIV

A semicircle of sheer, tan, rock walls rimmed the basin where we camped last night. Lush green grass carpeted the meadow and extended up the steep slope to the cliffs. An "avalanche chute" cut an ominous, jagged, gray scar that split the mountain from top to bottom. Dwight Creek meandered through the meadow before splashing over the edge and dropping down the steep mountainside into the valley miles below. The sun had already risen, and it promised to provide abundant heat even though we were in high country. I glanced at my watch. Eight o'clock and we hadn't even finished packing the mules. We were running late.

I led Amos, a flat- or "slab"-sided black mule, between two packs that lay on the ground five feet apart. Darrin, one of the wranglers, untied the sling ropes on the packsaddle. Amos leaned into my fingers

0

as I scratched his neck. "You're such a sweet mule. That's why you're the lead." Behind me I heard hooves swishing through long grass. I turned. My boss for this trip, Bill, approached, followed by a line of mounted guests. He guided his horse next to me and stopped. Raising his hand to block the sun from his eyes, he said, "I'm taking the guests and going ahead."

I nodded and yawned. Even though I'd rolled out of bed a couple of hours ago, I felt like I could crawl back into my sleeping bag for another 12 hours. All of us on crew were exhausted from the 18- to 20-hour days of hard physical labor that it took to run the summer pack trips. I shook my head to clear the sleepies. Whenever Bill left, he always told me the directions to the next campsite. If I'd have known what was going to happen in the next couple hours, I would've listened more carefully and taken notes. Instead I apathetically watched him as he pointed up a slope above the camp and said, "When you leave camp, I want you to be in front of both Darrin's string and Brett's."

Even though I was looking at him, all I heard was "Blah, blah, blah." I stretched and watched Darrin pick up a mantied pack—a wooden box that held eggs and produce. He heaved it onto Amos' packsaddle and nimbly tightened the sling rope that held the pack to the saddle. Yawning again, I noted Bill's lips were still moving. "Blah, blah, blah." Darrin tied off the pack and walked around to the other side of the mule. He heaved on another box.

Bill's horse bobbed its head and jigged in place, impatient to get on the trail. Its master reined it in and said, "It's a long, tough ride today. You'll need to hustle."

I nodded.

The boss tightened down his black cowboy hat and yelled to the other wrangler, who was loading mules with duffels, "Brett, have a good trip." Bill turned his horse up the slope and yelled back to me, "We'll see you on top—for lunch." He nodded at the guests. "Let's roll! We're burning daylight."

The guests, astride their horses, worked their way up the slope after Bill.

Darrin tied the sling rope in place. "Let's get these mules lined out and hit the trail." We spent the next 15 minutes tying the mules together, forming two pack strings of nine mules each. After Darrin mounted his horse, he guided it over to me. I handed him Amos' lead rope and then ambled through the knee-deep grass to my bay gelding, Czar. Behind me I heard Brett exclaim, "Oh, no! I don't believe it!"

I turned and watched him kick the toe of his boot in the dirt next to a little buckskin mule. Brett bent over and picked up a mule shoe. He held it in the air. "Pugmeyer lost a shoe."

Darrin and I responded in unison, "Not Pugmeyer!" My body sagged. "Oh-h-h." Pugmeyer was a skittish little mule that didn't want anyone messing with him, especially his feet. I grimaced. "We're going over the top today. The trail's too rocky to leave him barefoot."

Brett stroked his dark moustache and sighed. "I know. I'll tack it on. But we're going to be really late. Bill will be worried about us."

Soon the sun was scorching us. Beads of sweat dripped off Brett's forehead as he cautiously hammered the last nail in the mule's shoe. An hour had slipped past before I handed Amos' lead rope to Darrin, whose eyebrows creased as he said, "Bill's going to be worried sick. We need to make some good time on the trail."

I hustled over to Czar. The saddle creaked as I stepped up. Gathering the reins, I looked up the steep, grassy slope. *Now, where were we supposed to go?* Glancing at the sun I shook my head. *We'd better get moving.* As I nudged Czar forward, a thought scratched inside me: *Maybe I should ride ahead and check out the trail.* I tucked that thought under my cowboy hat and reasoned, *The trail can't be that hard to find, Bill just rode up the slope. I'll look for his tracks.*

Spotting a narrow dirt path with fresh horse tracks, I reined Czar onto it, but after a few feet the tracks disappeared. I wandered around again until I saw a hoofprint that glistened in some mud next to Dwight Creek. Leaning out of my saddle, I followed the tracks 100 yards then they vanished. Stopping, I cast my eyes to-and-fro. *Nothing.* My saddle creaked as I turned around and asked Darrin, "Did you hear what Bill said when he left camp?"

Darrin shook his head. "I thought you were listening," he said.

Mentally I kicked myself. *Why didn't I listen?* We snaked across the steep slope walking single file: first me, and then Darrin leading his string, and finally Brett with his string. My eyes caught a glimpse of some grass that was bent over. I slowed Czar to a crawl as I tracked Bill and the guests over to the avalanche chute, which was four feet deep and cut down the mountain. Last week's rain had created a miniature mud slide in the bottom of it. Bill's tracks followed the left edge of the chute. The trail turned straight up the mountain.

Guiding Czar, I leaned forward, urging him on. He labored up the steep trail. Behind me the mules' hooves clattered on the rocks. They were breathing hard as their packs pressed backward and the breast collars that helped hold the loads in place tightened. After 20 feet, I glanced at the trail again. No tracks. *Why didn't I listen to Bill?* I thought again. *Now we're perched on the side of this mountain, and I don't know where to go!* Czar continued to climb. Leaning forward again, I looked under my arm and saw Darrin's horse struggling uphill behind me. Frowning, I said, "I just lost Bill's tracks. Keep your eyes peeled."

Ahead of us, some tag alder brush formed a 10-foot wall on our left. It funneled us next to the chute. Deep inside my spirit, something itched again. *I don't like how close we're walking to the edge of this chute.* But instead of listening, I pushed the thought aside. In a few steps I spotted a downed log. The blood drained out of my face. A tree had fallen into the chute. It crossed the trail diagonally, forming a two-foot-high fence. I gulped. *If we were on a flat, the horses and mules could easily step over that...but we're headed straight uphill.*

I slowed Czar, and he walked up to the log and carefully lifted his feet. One by one, they scraped over the bark on the log. Walking him forward, I turned in my saddle to keep an eye on Darrin and his string.

Darrin's horse slowly stepped over. Darrin turned to watch his mules. Amos lifted his right front foot over, then his left front. Straddling the log, he picked up his right hind foot to step over. Suddenly the mule behind him threw up its head and hauled back. Its lead rope, which was tied to Amos' saddle, snapped tight and jerked Amos backward.

I watched in horror as the next few minutes unfolded in slow motion.

Amos' right hind foot fell into the chute, causing him to tip backward. Straining to get his balance forward, he desperately dug his feet into the trail, his right hind foot swinging in the air. Watching Amos flail, the mule behind freaked out. It reared up and threw its head, trying to break free and dragging Amos backward some more. I gasped as Amos' left hind foot skidded to the edge of the chute. Rocks crumbled off the edge. Amos dug in and braced himself against the tension of the rope.

The mule behind Amos sat on his haunches and snapped his head back and forth. Pop. The breakaway broke. With the release of tension, Amos' body flew forward. His front right foot fell into the chute. His body started to roll to the right. Amos grunted and heaved himself to the left. Overcompensating, his body twisted and reared. Standing on his hind legs, he pawed the air, frantically flailing. Slowly the weight of his packs shifted, pulling him backward and to the right. With a crash he toppled upside down into the chute. The chute was barely wide enough for his packs and the width of his body. He slid down the mountain—head first—the rocks grinding underneath him—all four feet churning the air. Finally and thankfully, his packs lodged tightly in the chute.

The mule that had been behind Amos stood on the edge of the chute and snorted. It whipped around and stampeded into the mules behind him, scaring them. In a chain reaction, Darrin's entire string churned and snorted until it became a tangled mass of mules.

Brett, Darrin, and I looked at each other, horror gripping our faces. Cold sweat dripped down my back. Tying a knot in my reins, I leaped off Czar and yelled, "Darrin, sort out your string, tie it to the back of Brett's. Tie your horse at the end. And hustle. We've got to get Amos on his feet before his guts push all the air out of his lungs. He's got about five minutes before he'll suffocate."

Crashing through the brush, Brett turned his mules downhill. I yelled, "Brett, take them down to the trees and tie up."

Running to the edge of the bank I stared at Amos. He was lying still. His black belly flinched as he grunted. Mud from the bottom of the chute oozed up around him. I pulled my knife out of its sheath. *I've got to cut that load and saddle off so he can get up.* I looked for a safe place to stand where I could reach Amos and the ropes. I didn't dare crawl into the chute below him because he might struggle, slide loose, and skid over the top of me. I glanced at the chute above him. *If I crawl in and he struggles, he'll bludgeon me with his hooves or he might impale himself on my knife.* The same was true if I squatted on either side of the bank and leaned over him. *God, how do I get him out?*

Panting from running uphill, Darrin walked next to me and pulled out his knife.

I looked at him. "Any ideas? It doesn't look good."

The whites of Amos' eyes showed. His nostrils flared. His breathing was growing shallow as his weight pressed against his lungs. Suddenly he gathered his strength, grunted again, and tried to turn upright. His body rocked; his feet flailed. He slid a few more inches down the chute. The egg boxes on each side of the pack wedged him in tighter. Amos panted and moaned.

Darrin chewed his cheek.

I paced along the chute, my mind racing through ideas. *I can't get in there to cut anything. The chute is so narrow and deep that the packs have him wedged.*

Amos grunted. His body rocked as he once again arched his neck and churned his feet. Fiercely he struggled. He slid down a couple more inches. Mud oozed around his head and the packs.

I rubbed my forehead. *He's only got a couple more minutes! With his head downhill I can't rope his front feet and use a horse to pull him uphill because it would break his legs or shoulders. And I can't rope his hind feet and pull them over his head because it'd fold him in half and break his neck.*

I wiped my sweaty palms on my jeans and looked hopelessly at Darrin.

Darrin's eyes brimmed with compassion. He shook his head and said, "Got a sky crane?"

I nervously giggled. *Sky crane. Lord, I don't have a sky crane, but You do. You have strong ministering angels ready to serve You. Please send them to flip Amos onto his feet.*

The brush rattled as Brett stormed up. Panting, he stood on the edge of the chute next to us and surveyed the situation. Amos' belly barely moved now. Brett took off his hat and ran his hand through his dark hair.

Suddenly Amos curled his back, folding his feet together. He grunted and rocked.

All three of us backed away.

I shook my head as I looked at the poor mule. Slowly he lifted his head and then moved it up and down. He rocked, grunted, and heaved. Suddenly mud sprayed everywhere. Amos' rear-end flipped over his head and downhill. He was up on his feet! Mud dripped off the packs and down his sides. From the top of his long ears all the way down to his hooves he was caked in goo. He propped his legs at angles to hold his exhausted body upright.

The three of us whooped and danced. We cheered and slapped high-fives. Sliding into the chute, we gently hugged Amos. His head hung low as he took long, deep breaths. With my finger I traced the cowlick on his muddy forehead. "I'm so sorry, Amos," I whispered. Stroking his neck, I heaved a relieved sigh.

I'd almost gotten Amos killed because of my apathetic attitude. First, I hadn't paid attention when Bill gave me his instructions. Then I did the same thing when God whispered in my spirit about finding and checking the trail before we'd started out. And when He'd warned me again about riding too close to the ditch, all I allowed myself to hear was "Blah, blah, blah." The reason God and Bill had given me directions was to protect me. *How can they protect me if I keep ignoring them?* I wondered.

I patted Amos' forehead and whispered, "I'm going to listen next time."

Yellow goo dripped from the packs. Brett wiped it with a finger and looked at it closely. "Eggs broke," he observed.

We all chuckled nervously, still in shock from the near tragedy.

A chunk of mud fell out of Amos' ear, and we burst out laughing.

Then I had a horrible thought. With wide eyes I looked at Brett and Darrin, "What are we going to tell Bill?"

"Maybe he won't notice," Brett offered jokingly.

Darrin folded his knife and slid it into its sheath. "We could say that a mudslide rushed down the mountain and swept Amos away, hopelessly wedging him upside down..."

I giggled and looked toward heaven and finished his thought, "Until a sky crane appeared and pulled him out."

To this day I'm convinced that God sent His helpers to catapult Amos out of that chute. It was a true miracle that he'd survived and hadn't broken his neck when he somersaulted.

> *Lord, forgive me when apathy takes over and I choose to ignore You and the people You've put in my life to help me and guide me. Give me the wisdom and energy to listen, even when I'm tired or distracted. Amen.*

9

Bobbing for Apples

*Fix your thoughts on what is true, and honorable,
and right, and pure, and lovely,
and admirable. Think about things that are
excellent and worthy of praise.*

Philippians 4:8 nlt

I peered out the window that overlooked the horse pasture and ogled my new majestic Tennessee walker. Her black coat glimmered blue in the sunlight, and her long, black tail flowed to the ground. She was worthy to be in a king's stable, and here she was in mine. I still couldn't believe it.

Only hours ago I'd unloaded her from the horse trailer. With an arched neck and a composed, stately manner, she explored her new domain, sniffing around the barn and corral. Now she was strolling around the water tank. She nuzzled the sides and lightly chewed on the top edge. Making a scooping motion with her head, she splashed water over the side. She smelled the water on the ground and pawed the newly created mud. Stepping next to the tank, she dunked her head—all the way up to her eyes.

I pushed my nose against the window, shocked. She pulled her head out and shook the water off her nose. Then she plunged her head in again...way past her ears. I'd never seen a horse do anything like this. I'd never even heard of a horse doing this. *What's wrong?* I worried.

I flew out the door. My boots pounded down the dirt trail, and I squeezed through the fence. My new mare ambled over to greet me, water dripping off her chin. I scratched her soggy forehead and asked, "Are you feeling okay?" My mind whirled. *Does she have a fever?* I felt her throat. She wasn't sweaty or clammy. Puzzled, I perched on the edge of the water tank and watched her for a while. She seemed normal.

Just as I turned to go she lumbered to the water tank, pawed the mud with her front foot, and then submerged her entire head in the water. She must have gone all the way to the bottom of the tank! It looked like she was bobbing for apples. *There's something really wrong. Horses don't do this!*

I ran to the house and called the previous owner. "Connie, I think there's something wrong! The mare's acting really strange." I quickly explained what was happening.

Connie laughed. "It's okay, Rebecca. There's nothing to worry about. She's dunking her head all the way to the bottom so she can pull out the drain plug. She wants the water to run out onto the ground so she can play in the puddle."

Relieved, I laughed. "Ah! I bought a horse with a sense of humor. She'll fit right in around here!"

Lord, help me to remember that when I jump to conclusions,
I should first jump to positive ones. Amen.

10

Picket Rope

An evil man is held captive by his own sins;
they are ropes that catch and hold him.

PROVERBS 5:22 NLT

The sound of chainsaws whined through the May morning air. D.J. and Richard sawed the dilapidated wood rail fence into fire-sized pieces. I picked up the chunks and stacked them on the woodpile next to the campfire. For the last couple weeks the crew had been tearing down and rebuilding the corrals at the trailhead.

Taking a break, I grabbed a couple of plastic glasses from under the green kitchen tarp and picked up the pitcher of Kool-Aid. I waved it in the air to catch the attention of the other crew members. Richard saw me and set down the chainsaw. He wiped his brow and motioned to D.J. I sat on a campstool next to the fire as they sauntered over, helped themselves to the Kool-Aid, and got comfortable.

Tucking a long strand of blond hair behind my ear, I asked, "Where's Danny?"

With his cup of Kool-Aid in hand, Richard pointed toward the back pasture. "I sent him over by the creek to pull down barbed wire."

I nodded. "Good. We don't need him anywhere near the chain-saws." Joy rushed through me. I felt like I was a part of the "in" crowd as I went on, "Not after he dropped that tree down on the fence line. How can anybody be so stupid?" No sooner were the words out of my mouth when I felt a twinge in my spirit...but I ignored it.

Richard and D.J. scowled at the memory of the tree falling. It had destroyed a week's worth of jack-leg fence building.

D.J. poked the fire with a stick. Taking a candy bar out of his pocket, he tapped it on his leg. He gritted his teeth. "He'd better stay away from my stash. If he steals a candy bar like he did last week, I'll..."

I rocked back on my camp stool, adding, "And keep him away from the gas cans!" A couple days ago when we were burning slash piles, one of the fires smoldered for hours. All of us on crew watched in horror as Danny picked up a gas can, walked over to the fire, and poured gas directly onto the small flame. The flame whooshed up the gas and into the can. We screamed, "Run!" expecting an explosion any second. We dove under the horse trailer for cover, but Danny slowly set the can on the ground, bent over, and blew out the flame in the can.

I shook my head. "The guy must be mentally challenged." The smoke from the fire drifted my direction. My eyes watered. Once again an ugly feeling choked my spirit. Once again I pushed it aside. Fanning the smoke I stood up. "I'm going to go picket Dusty."

I led the chocolate-colored gelding to a small grassy spot. Holding on to his lead rope, I picked up a hobble I'd brought and held it toward Dusty. "You know what this is," I said. He reached his muzzle toward it and sniffed. I scratched his forehead. "Today you get to learn about being on a picket rope." Dusty leaned into my fingers and moved his head up and down so I would scratch his forehead.

I leaned down and strapped the hobble to his left front leg and snapped the picket rope to the hobble's ring. Standing and facing him, I urged him forward. When he lifted his left front foot, the picket rope swished through the grass. Dusty glanced sideways. I stopped him. "Good boy. Now, that's not too scary, is it?" I clucked for him to move forward again. Keeping an eye on the rope that slithered beside him like a snake, he hesitantly moved forward. I stopped him again and rubbed his neck. "You're going to get the hang of this in no time." After a few more steps, Dusty didn't bother looking at the rope. Instead he eyed the green grass.

I walked him in a circle a few times with the rope trailing behind. He acted like he was an old pro, so I slipped the other end of the picket rope over the picket pin I'd pounded into the earth. I led him forward until the slack was out of the rope. I clucked for him to take one more step. As he lifted his left front foot the rope grew taut. He pulled against the rope. I tapped the lead rope and asked him to back up. He set his foot down and backed up, relieving the pressure on his foot. I rubbed his neck again as I reassured him. "See that's not too bad. When you get to the end of the rope, just back up." I walked him around the 40-foot circle, leading him to the end of the rope a couple more times. As soon as he felt the pressure from the rope, he stopped and backed up. Slipping off the halter, I said, "I'll be keeping an eye on you. Enjoy the grass." I strolled back to help the guys stack wood. During the next hour, we continued to tell all the "stupid Danny stories" we knew. The more we told, the more worked up we became. My spirit felt nauseous, and I knew I was being ugly and cruel. I justified it by noting, *This guy deserves it. Besides, I've got to blow off steam somehow.*

I glanced at Dusty peacefully grazing. In a couple weeks we were planning on using him on a summer pack trip, so he needed to learn about being picketed. *I might as well turn the other horses and mules loose with him,* I decided. I slid open the wood rails to the small corral. The horses and mules spurted out at a trot. Dusty calmly watched. In minutes they all had their heads down munching grass. Over the next couple hours they milled around Dusty, who didn't seem to mind being on the picket.

Suddenly a couple of the horses jerked up their heads and spun around, their nostrils flared and the whites of their eyes showed. Shading my eyes against the sun with my hand, I squinted into the woods where they were looking. I didn't see anything. The rest of the herd lifted their heads, their ears perked forward, their nostrils flaring to catch any scent. Suddenly the lead mare, a bay, spun and plunged forward, smashing into the horse next to her. That horse jumped sideways like she'd gotten bitten and then raced full blast smack dab into the rest of the herd.

The horses milled around and crashed into each other before grouping to follow the lead mare. In a couple steps they accelerated to what seemed like mach 10 and thundered toward Dusty. I wanted to cover my eyes. I knew what was about to happen, and it wasn't going to be pretty. At a dead run the herd rushed past Dusty. He turned with them and took off. In two strides he was running all out. I cringed. Within seconds he was at the end of the rope. Thwack! The rope held fast to his left front leg and the picket stake. The momentum of his body flipped him in a somersault. Wham! His back slammed against the ground. A cloud of dust billowed, and Dusty lay still. I was sure he'd broken his leg at the very least.

I ran to the horse's side. Dusty's chest rose and fell in fits as he gasped for air. He rolled his big brown eyes as he looked up at me. Lifting his head, he groaned as he suddenly rocked to his feet, shook, and nudged me. I breathed a sigh of relief and stroked his forehead. "See what happens when you join the crowd?" I whispered. Then I gasped as my spirit realized what I'd said. Here I'd been bad-mouthing Danny because it made me feel like I belonged to the "in" crowd. I knew it was wrong to gossip, even if somebody did crazy, stupid things. That ugly feeling was my conscience tugging on me, just like that picket rope did for Dusty. I felt like I'd flipped over as I stroked Dusty's neck and commented, "I've learned something today too."

Danny worked for the outfit for a few more months. Although he continued to goof up, I quit making fun of him. Instead I coached him and tried to help him along. Sometimes he listened, but most of the time he didn't. But the important thing was that I was reaching out and doing the right thing.

> *Lord, give me the strength to stand on my own and do what's right, whether I'm leading or following. Show me how to be part of Your crowd. Amen.*

11

Liquid Brand

My son, keep my words, and
treasure my commands within you.

PROVERBS 7:1

Behind me the guests rode their horses single file down the dusty trail that wound through the pines. It was the first day of a summer pack trip, and already the hot July sun had burned my arms. My saddle creaked as I turned around and hollered, "Time for a lunch break. Tie up your horses, grab your lunches, and let's eat by the creek." I stepped out of the saddle and tied Sunrise, my palomino mare, to a tree. When I pulled out the water bottle and the brown lunch sack from my saddle bags, a Ziploc bag filled with 3 x 5 cards fell on the ground. *Oops! I forgot to work on my Scripture memory verses—again!* I'd vowed to memorize Scripture during the summer, but it seemed like every time I remembered I had guests with me, I was too tired to keep my eyes open, or it was too dark to read.

I picked up the bag and stuffed it into the saddlebag. Julie walked up and patted Sunrise on the neck. She ran her hand down her shoulder and traced the brand with her fingers. "Why do you brand them? Doesn't it really hurt them?"

I buckled my saddlebags closed. "That one didn't hurt, but it's not a legal brand either."

Julie took off her black cowboy hat and tucked her mid-length brown hair behind her ears. She frowned.

"Are you confused?"

Julie grinned and nodded.

"It's a long story." The other guests joined us as we walked along the path toward the creek, moving through lodgepole pines. "It's important to brand horses when we're outfitting because every night we turn all but two of them loose to graze. We choose a large meadow, perhaps a mile long that has natural barriers, such as rock walls or trees. Let me show you." I bent over, picked up a stick, and in the dusty trail I drew a large oval with a line through it. "A trail runs through the meadow. At either end a wrangler pickets his saddle horse and sets up his wickiup, a small tarp he stretches between two trees to protect him from the dew and possible rainfall while he sleeps. Before we turn the herd loose, we buckle a bell on the lead horse. Have you seen those big old cowbells?"

The guests nodded.

I straightened. "That's what the ones we use look like. You can hear the bell, da-ding da-ding, da-ding, a long ways away. Because these critters walk on trails all day through the mountains, that's what they do at night if they decide to travel."

The guests and I sat down on a grassy bank above the creek, dangling our legs over the chortling water. We opened our lunch sacks. I pulled out a ham sandwich and took a bite before continuing. "If the herd wanders by the wrangler, he's supposed to hear the bell and wake up. He then gets up and pushes the herd back into the meadow. Occasionally there will be a wandering mountain lion, grizzly bear, or a "bogeyman," who'll get the horses riled up. Our bogeyman isn't really anything scary. He might be something as silly as a squirrel that drops a pinecone and startles the horses. They freak out and take off. Sometimes when that happens the horses and mules stampede past the groggy wrangler. He has to quickly saddle his horse and chase after them."

The guests listened intently. Julie stared at me, her brown eyes wide. "What if he doesn't find them?"

"The rest of the wranglers quickly join in the search. Using flashlights, they can track the main herd pretty easy. If a couple of the horses do something out of the ordinary, such as take a different fork in the trail and get separated from the herd, that can be a problem. This Bob Marshall Wilderness Complex is so vast that they could wander 100 miles or so before anybody might come across them. That's where the brand comes in."

I dipped my hand into my sack and pulled out a Butterfinger candy bar. The wrapper crinkled as I peeled it back. "All Montana brands are issued and registered by the state to an individual. The individual 'owns' his brand. And each brand is different. It can be letters, numbers, and signs, such as a straight line that is referred to as a bar. The items can also be stacked vertically or horizontally. But there's more to the brand than the symbols. Part of the registration includes the brand location. So every brand has a specific place on the animals, depending on who owns the brand.

"For instance, our outfit's brand is only valid if it's located on the right front shoulder of our horses and mules. If the same grouping of symbols appears on a different part of the animals, such as the right thigh, it belongs to someone else."

I tilted my hat to block the sun. Picking up my water bottle, I unscrewed the top and tipped the container into my mouth. Cool, refreshing water rolled down my throat. "A brand is equivalent to the owner's signature. So the moral of the story is 'Don't mess with someone else's livestock because in the state of Montana horse thieving is still on the books as a hanging offense.'"

Julie cocked her head. "You're kidding, right?"

"Nope."

She reached into her lunch sack. Pulling out a 3 Musketeers bar, she pointed it at me. "Aren't you worried then? You said the brand on Sunrise isn't legal."

The guests leaned forward, so quiet I could've heard a twig snap.

I swallowed the last bite of my Butterfinger. "I'm not worried at all. Her brand is where it's supposed to be…and it's the right symbols, but the method of placing it there is counterfeit."

"Why?"

"When it came time to brand, my boss didn't want to hurt the horses. Not realizing it wasn't legal, he used a chemical branding process. He dipped the iron brand into a special solution and then held it against the horse. Instead of burning the brand on, like is traditionally done, the chemical scorches the hair follicles so the horse would be bald where the chemical touched. Unfortunately, that doesn't count under current Montana state law."

I stuffed the candy wrapper into my sack. "Back in the old days when cattle rustling was a lot more common, thieves would round up herds and rebrand by adding additional letters. The 'new' brand would be registered to them so they could claim the herd as their own. The only way to prove that rebranding had occurred was to kill one of the cows and skin it. From the backside of the hide, the original brand shows as dominant, making the alterations clear. So a brand in this state isn't legal unless the animal has a brand seared on its hide so it will show up if there's a dispute. The only way to get that type of brand is with a heated branding iron. It does hurt the animal for a short while, but the wound heals in a couple of days. Without that type of branding, there's no way to secure ownership."

"I understand now," Julie said. "Thanks."

I looked at the guests. "Grab your stuff. It's time to hit the trail."

When I walked up to Sunrise, I looked at her brand. *Most people would never guess it's a counterfeit.* I unbuckled my saddlebags and stuffed in my empty lunch sack and water bottle. As I pushed aside the Ziploc bag filled with Scripture cards I realized that the primary purpose for memorizing them was to brand God's Word on my heart. *It's like a brand of ownership.* The pain of learning them would only "sting" for a few days. The benefits would last a lifetime. I pulled out the Ziploc, untied Sunrise, and swung into the saddle. *I bet I can learn a couple of these this afternoon while riding.*

Lord, I don't want to be a counterfeit in Your kingdom. Please give me a passion to sear Your Word into my heart. Amen.

12

A Helping Hand

*Don't worry about anything; instead,
pray about everything. Tell God what you need,
and thank him for all he has done.*

PHILIPPIANS 4:6 CEV

U nder the pines in the Danaher Valley, dozens of horses and mules stood tied to the rope corral as the wranglers pulled off packs and saddles. The August afternoon heat and the smell of animal sweat lured droning horseflies. The stock switched their tails and stomped their feet to shake off the hungry flies. A tall, raw-boned, cinnamon-colored Appaloosa with no mane and a rat-tail stood tied at the end of the row. She was a backcountry trail expert, having gone on hundreds of pack trips. Her ribs were showing from all the hard work this trip and not quite enough feed.

I took off my hat and ran my fingers through my hair. *What am I going to do about Melinda?* At the beginning of this trip she'd looked fine. But the last five days of grueling mountain trails combined with four nights on a picket rope sheered the weight off her. I had to keep her on the picket rope because she was totally night-blind. *She needs more feed than she can get staked on a picket.* We didn't have any grain left, we were miles from supplies, and there were five more days left before getting to base camp. *What can I do?*

Melinda was an unusual horse because anybody—guest or crew—could ride her. Gentle even as a newborn filly, Melinda "walked out" on the trail, stood politely while being mounted, and responded to the lightest touch on the reins. She loved going on the trips so we took her on almost every one.

Melinda stomped, protesting a biting fly. The muscles rippled over her ribs. *You are too thin.* At night on summer trips we turned the horses and mules loose to graze, using the folds of the mountains and the thick forest as a natural corral. *She needs to be turned out with the herd to graze all night.*

Melinda rubbed a fly from her face. *She really needs that feed now. I have to do it.*

I hollered to a wrangler, "Brian, turn Melinda loose tonight."

"But she's…"

"I know. But she needs the feed. If you turn the herd out now instead of after dinner, we can keep an eye on her." I slipped on my hat and walked to the kitchen tarp where the guests were filling their plates with tossed salad and spaghetti. I grabbed a plate of food and, instead of joining them, carried it and my steaming coffee out to the meadow. Sitting against a tree, I watched Melinda and mentally beat myself up. *What was I thinking, turning her loose?* I stabbed the noodles with my fork. *After dark, if the herd moves faster than a walk, will she be able to keep up? Will she panic and take off—running blind? Maybe right off a cliff? And with the whole herd following? Should I put her on a picket rope after all?* As the sun sank, the shadows exaggerated Melinda's ribs. I weakly surrendered. *God, You know Melinda needs the feed. Please watch over her tonight.* But I was haunted by worry for Melinda…and God. *Am I doing the right thing? And should I bother such a busy God by asking Him to watch over a horse?*

As the sun slid behind the snowcapped peaks, casting golden-pink shadows across the grass, Melinda walked over to Roman, a sorrel mule with a white mane that was roached—cut short. Puzzled I thought, *How odd. Our horses don't usually care for mules.* When twilight settled over the valley and the moon rose, Roman picked up his head and chortled to Melinda. Melinda walked over and positioned herself behind him. Then she did an incredibly strange thing—she rested her head on Roman's rump. Like a truck hitched to a gooseneck trailer, they lumbered through the moonlit meadow. When Roman smelled a delicious spot, he stopped and cropped grass. Melinda did too. When Roman was ready to move, he lifted his head and called for Melinda. Once again she'd rest her head on his rump and they wandered off. *How amazing! He's acting as her seeing-eye dog. It's a miracle! Only You, God, could make this happen.*

God isn't too busy. He *did* care about that raw-boned, rat-tailed horse in the boonies. He *did* care about my concerns. Grabbing my plate and cup, I strolled toward the guests huddled around the crackling campfire. I knew Melinda was safe.

Whenever I think God's too busy or my requests too trivial, I remember that night in the valley. And I'm reminded that He cares about everything; He's just waiting for me to ask.

> *Thank You, Lord, for being an almighty God who wants to help me with every detail of my life. Give me the courage to turn my cares over to You so I don't worry about anything. Amen.*

13

Breakaway

A person standing alone can be attacked and defeated,
but two can stand back-to-back and conquer.
Three are even better, for a
triple-braided cord is not easily broken.

Ecclesiastes 4:12 nlt

A lone owl hooted in the night. The horses and mules munched hay in the wooden corral at Monture Creek Camp. Richard, D.J., and I sat next to a crackling campfire. The light flickered across our faces as each of us bent over a breakaway, a six-inch circle of braided rope we held in our laps. A pile of breakaways lay on the ground. We were cutting one strand of rope out of each one.

The prickly manila strands had rubbed my fingers raw. I placed the rope between my thumb and first finger of my right hand. Pushing with my thumb, I untwisted the three plies of rope by rolling my first finger backward. The rope was so stiff it felt like I was separating metal cable strands. I twisted my fingers even harder. As the plies separated, a small loop formed in the rope. When I slipped my index finger in the loop, the prickly rope ripped my cuticle open. Blood oozed out. "Ouch!" I muttered.

Richard and D.J. glanced at me.

I wiped the blood off my finger. "What a pain. It took us two weeks around the campfire—every evening—to braid these pieces of rope into circles." I stuck my pocketknife into the loop and sawed to cut out a single ply. "And now we've got to cut out one strand so they'll break easier. Who would have thought ¼-inch manila rope would be so strong?"

The smoke of the fire shifted and enveloped D.J. He fanned it with his cowboy hat and scooted sideways. "I never thought I'd see that little black mule straddle a tree," he commented.

My memory conjured up a picture of the mule as I unwound the single strand. *I hope I never see that again. I can't believe she didn't get killed.* Today I'd learned the importance of having a breakaway...that breaks. Although the six-inch circle of rope looked insignificant, it was one of the most important pieces of equipment on a pack trip. There's one breakaway fastened onto the back of each packsaddle. The mule that walks behind this saddle is tied by its lead rope to the breakaway. Its purpose is to break under sudden pressure, so if a mule loses its footing or falls off a cliff, it doesn't drag the rest of the string down. With the breakaways, the mules can be tied single file behind each other with a "safety valve" between them. This makes handling them on the trail a lot easier and safer.

Today we'd each pulled a string of nine mules loaded with mantied hay bales into camp. D.J.'s popper, the end mule, was named Hawks. She hadn't been paying attention. When the mules had plodded on the right side of a tree in the trail, Hawks was eating green shoots of grass on her way around the left side of the tree. When the rope pulled tight against the tree, instead of giving in to the pressure and backing up, she did what all mules do—she slammed her 850 pounds forward, trying to break the rope. The rope peeled the bark off the tree and jerked the mule to which Hawks was tied backward. The mule in front did what mules do—it goosed forward—against the pressure—and slammed into the mule in front of it. The rope seesawed against the tree as the mules fought against the rope.

Hawks reared up, lost her footing, and fell forward onto a stubby pine tree that had rooted on the edge of the trail. She straddled that sagging pine tree. The lead rope somehow wrapped around the spindly tree a couple of times and yet still held fast to the breakaway on the saddle of the mule in front of her. The rope was tight between them. Under the weight of Hawks, the mule in front dug all four hooves into the trail to keep from slipping backward. At the same time, the whole string exploded. Mules squealed and dirt flew. Not one of the breakaways did its job. When the dust settled, the string of mules was tangled up like a pile of worms, and Hawks dangled over the edge.

D.J. jumped out of his saddle and did the only thing he could. He cut the breakaway tying Hawks to the mule in front of him. Hawks tumbled down the slope, a pile of rocks clattering down behind her. At the bottom, she thrashed around until she got her feet underneath her. Standing up, she shook herself. Miraculously she was fine, but it took hours before we got the mules untangled, the loads straightened out, and Hawks back up on the trail. The wreck wouldn't have happened if the breakaway had done what it was supposed to do.

The campfire popped, spitting a cluster of miniature fires toward Richard. He scooted backward and swept dirt over them. "Who would've thought that three small strands of rope could hold that much weight?"

I sawed my knife against another strand. "Three strands" echoed through my mind. It reminded me of the Bible verse about the three-ply cord that was not easily broken. I thought of that in reference to prayer. *To pray in Jesus' name is a two-ply cord made up of Jesus and me. More powerful was agreement in prayer with another person and Jesus. Hmmm. Yesterday my friend Joan and I had prayed for our safety…as well as the safety of the stock on this trip. That's why Hawks is fine.* Glancing through the column of smoke I said, "The strength of three strands *is* amazing, isn't it?"

From that day on, Hawks followed the mule in front of her. She was never caught on the wrong side of a tree again. And I started regularly using the three-strand cord—the power of praying in agreement with my friends.

Lord, thank You for showing me Your prayer equation: agreement with another person plus Your presence equals strength. Amen.

14

Callused, Cracked, and Bleeding

*This people's heart has become calloused;
they hardly hear with their ears, and
they have closed their eyes. Otherwise they might
see with their eyes, hear with their ears,
understand with their hearts
and turn, and I would heal them.*

MATTHEW 13:15

Lodgepole pine trees blanketed the rolling mountains. The dusty trail wound through gullies, across hillsides, and through corridors of pines. The morning breeze whispered through the pine needles, carrying a hint of fresh snow from the high country. Today the horse I was riding was green (inexperienced). I was pulling a string of nine mules loaded with hay to Monture Creek Camp. After riding the 14 miles to camp, I would drop the hay off, turn around, and ride the 14 miles back to the trailhead.

Amarillo, my copper-colored gelding, jerked his head sideways, pulling loose a couple inches of rein. He lurched forward, quickening his step. But the mule behind me, whose lead rope I held in my right hand, kept walking at the same pace. In two steps my right arm was almost jerked out of its socket. I was stretched between my horse and the mule. I didn't dare let go of the lead rope because the mules might take off or get wound up and have a wreck. My left hand scrambled for the reins. I drew back on them, saying, "Slow down, boy."

Amarillo arched his neck and pranced sideways.

"Stop it!" I growled. The muscles in my outstretched arm screamed. I tugged the reins until my horse stopped. Pulling on the lead rope, I reeled in the mule. "I wish Sunrise..." Tears welled in the corner of my eyes. I corralled my emotions and herded my thoughts another direction.

I glanced at my hand holding the lead rope. Blood dripped from my knuckles. At the beginning of every season, the skin on my hands forms new calluses. The spring wind and rain chaps them, so when I bump them or apply a lot of pressure like hauling on a lead rope, the skin cracks and bleeds. I winced as I wiped away the blood. *I need to smear them with Corn Huskers lotion tonight.*

This lotion is unique and wonderful. Most of us on the ranch use it. Other lotions soften hands by removing the calluses, so our hands would be painful as calluses were built-up again. Then they would get chapped and break open and bleed, and we'd apply lotion...and it would begin again. But Corn Huskers didn't remove calluses, instead it was like a salve that made them pliable so they wouldn't crack and bleed.

Gently I squeezed my legs and urged Amarillo to take a baby step. Once again he lurched forward.

"Slow down, Amarillo!" I tugged him to a stop and reeled in the mule again. "Why did I choose to ride *you?* At this pace we'll never get to camp." *If I were riding Sunrise...* My heart shattered with the memory.

I'd put a solid season of training into Sunrise, a beautiful, cream-colored palomino mare. By late fall last year she'd become a great horse for pulling a string of pack mules. As soon as she felt any pressure from the lead mule or felt the lead rope pressure through me, she'd ease her pace. She also knew to slow down when we rode switchbacks. She'd become more than just a pleasure to ride. She was my partner. Her favorite thing was the extra peanut butter sandwich I packed in the saddlebags for *her* lunch.

My heart ached as I remembered bringing the herd home a month and a half ago from the winter pasture. She'd looked fat and sassy when she walked out of the stock truck and down the ramp. As the herd streamed onto the summer pasture, Sunrise ran along, kicking and bucking in high spirits as she joined them.

That night at ten thirty the phone blared. It was a rancher who lived on the back side of the pasture. "We were on our way home and one of your horses wouldn't get off the road. We slowed down. We couldn't figure out why it wouldn't move out of the headlights. When we got closer, we saw that it couldn't move. It had a broken leg. I think it got caught in the cattle guard. I'm sorry."

With a hollow thud I set down the phone, hoping it wasn't Sunrise. I woke the boss and told him one of the horses had a broken leg. He grabbed his .41 Ruger pistol and met me at the pickup. The headlights eerily cut through the black night as we bounced down the dirt road through the pasture. Soon we saw the outline of a horse.

When the horse recognized the sound of the truck, it whinnied and hobbled on three legs toward us. Its broken leg swung like a rope because it was shattered into so many pieces.

Then the headlights glinted off the cream-colored coat. I squeezed my eyes closed. Sunrise. We drove alongside her. I knew there was nothing that could be done. There wasn't anything left of the bone in her lower leg.

I've got to be strong. I bit my lip as I stepped out of the truck. "Hi, girl."

Sunrise nickered and shook her head as if to say, "I'm glad you're here. I'm so scared." She hobbled toward me.

The headlights shone on her long, black eyelashes that rimmed frightened brown eyes. I wrapped my arms around her neck. "I don't want to say goodbye. I love you." I buried my face into her soft fur and cried.

Releasing my grip, I stepped back. I held her face between my hands and kissed her forehead.

Metal clicked against metal as the boss loaded a bullet into the chamber.

I stepped back again.

I couldn't turn away. My eyes focused on her. The boss held the pistol to her head.

The pistol roared.

She fell with a hollow thud.

The roar of the shot echoed through my memory. I shook my head and came back to the present. Tears streamed down my face, and my nose dripped as I gathered the reins. *God, I hurt so badly. I loved her so much. I don't ever want to love another horse that much. Never again.*

I pulled a red bandana out of my back pocket and blew my nose. As I folded it, I looked at the deep and bloody cracks on my knuckles. *Lord, my knuckles look just like my heart feels: dried up, callused, broken open, and bleeding. Help me heal.*

Deep within my spirit I heard, "To be healed, you have to love again."

With each of Amarillo's footsteps I swayed in the saddle and sobbed. *Lord, I can't. It hurts too much.*

From my spirit I heard, "Love is like a salve. When you allow yourself to love again, the hurt doesn't go away; instead the new love keeps the past hurt from breaking open and bleeding. It helps those past hurts fade away."

Amarillo jerked his head sideways, trying to pull loose a couple inches of rein. I held them tight and rubbed his neck. "No, mister, you're not going to do that again. We're going to work on this thing one day at a time."

Over the next year Amarillo and I worked on becoming partners.

We hit a lot of walls, but by the time the leaves turned gold and littered the trail, I enjoyed pulling a mule string from Amarillo's back. I tried feeding him peanut butter sandwiches, but he never liked them. His favorite was leftover pancakes with maple syrup.

Lord, give me the courage to love again even though I've been hurt. Heal my heart so it will quit bleeding. Amen.

15

Hoof for Hoof

*Watch your step, and the road
will stretch out smooth before you.
Look neither right nor left; leave evil in the dust.*

PROVERBS 4:26-27 MSG

The ravens floated across the sky. I squinted and watched them lazily soaring over the ridge. Sweat dripped down my back from the hot August sun. It was the first day of a five-day summer pack trip. In front of me the long line of horses trudged single file through pines corridors. Dust boiled up from the trail with each horse's step. Sweat glistened from my bay gelding's neck. I stroked Czar's shoulder. "It's already a scorcher, and it's only eleven o'clock," I commented. The heat had driven the songbirds and squirrels into their shady nests, leaving the forest quiet. Quiet...except for the sound of horses' hooves hitting the trail...and Brad's chattering.

Brad, a sandy-brown-haired nine year old had once again returned with his family. He adored me, and the feeling was mutual. Brad rode directly in front of me. His saddle creaked as he wiggled and turned around. "Did I tell you what happened..." As Brad turned, he accidentally squeezed his legs together and pulled on the reins. Seagram, the brown mule he was riding, followed his cues and turned into the forest.

I waved toward the left. "Brad, watch where you're going!"

Brad straightened himself in the saddle and reined Seagram back to the trail. He turned around again. "And…" Once again he pushed with his legs and pulled the reins. Seagram dove into the trees.

I shook my head. "Brad, get her on the trail. If she winds through the woods she might squish your leg against a tree. That would hurt."

Brad shrugged his shoulders and reined her back onto the trail. The next couple miles he squirmed and fidgeted. Seagram walked like a drunk, weaving back and forth as Brad kept pulling the reins. The trail climbed uphill and then traversed across a hillside. Narrowing to only five-feet wide, on the left side of the trail the hill dropped down a steep grassy slope into a gully. The right side climbed straight up the mountain.

Seagram walked down the center of the trail with Brad humming and bouncing to his own tune. Suddenly the boy spotted something on the slope. I cringed as he leaned off the right side of the saddle, reaching for something. His movement pushed Seagram toward the drop-off. She scaled the edge of the trail. Stones clattered down the slope. I opened my mouth to yell at him just as Seagram's hind foot plunged off the trail. Stumbling forward, she caught her balance.

I rubbed my forehead and growled, "Brad, sit up in your saddle! You just about pushed your mule off the trail."

Brad straightened up, and Seagram drifted back to the center. But in a couple steps Brad draped his left arm over Seagram's neck and reached toward the slope. He plucked something and popped it into his mouth. I looked at the bushes. *The huckleberries are ripe.* Huckleberries are similar to blueberries. Because they were growing on the uphill slope, Brad could pick them from Seagram's back.

I chewed on my lip. "Brad, what did I just tell you?"

"But…"

"No buts. You could get hurt doing that." Taking a deep breath I continued. "I'll tell you what. I'll help you pick huckleberries when we stop for lunch. Now sit straight in your saddle. You need to make Seagram follow the horse in front of her—hoof for hoof."

Brad's shoulders slumped and his head bobbed with each of Seagram's steps. Seagram seemed relieved as she ambled down the trail, her long brown ears flopping gently. Then Brad wormed around once again. I threw my arms in the air and said, "Brad!"

He straightened back up again...and again...and again.

That night in camp, Brad shadowed me everywhere. After he helped me gather moss and sticks to start the fire, I ruffled his hair. "Brad, the only reason I scold you is because I've gotten hurt doing those same things, and I don't want you to get hurt. Do you understand?" Brad blinked his blue-green eyes and nodded. But the next five days Seagram wandered to-and-fro between trees and past huckleberry bushes with me shaking my finger and scolding her rider the whole way.

On the last morning of the trip we mounted up. I reined Czar into the lead. Brad fell in behind me, followed by the rest of the guests. The sun peaked from behind a mountain, casting golden rays like a crown. The animals ambled cross-country through scattered pines and a large meadow with knee-high grass that swayed in the cool breeze. Gradually the distance between each horse and mule spanned a few hundred yards. When I came to the trail, I reined Czar onto the dirt and listened for Seagram's hooves. But all I heard were her feet swishing through the grass. I turned and glanced at Brad, who leaned forward like a race car driver. With his reins gathered, he was weaving Seagram through the pines like they were flags on an obstacle course. I rolled my eyes. "Brad, get over here! Remember—hoof for hoof."

Brad kicked Seagram. They trotted onto the trail behind me. I relaxed in the saddle and watched the chickadees flit from pinecone to pinecone, pulling out the seeds and eating them. A couple of minutes later there was silence. I turned. Brad was weaving Seagram through the pines again. I frowned and pointed behind me. Kicking Seagram, they trotted into place.

As the sun rose, it cast shadows across the forest floor. Once again there was silence, and then the quick patter of Seagram's hooves as she trotted up behind me. Suddenly a blood-curdling scream shattered the morning. *Who could that be? Brad's right behind me.* I turned and looked back. Seagram was rambling down the trail...but without Brad. He wasn't in the saddle! I scanned the trail behind us. Nothing. The other guests were so far behind us I couldn't see them. I spun Czar around. My eyes shifted back and forth, scanning the ground. Nothing.

Brad screamed again. I nudged Czar forward, trying to locate him. The sound came from off the trail. I blinked and looked up. Brad was hanging upside down in a tree. *What on earth?*

I kicked Czar and galloped to the tree. Brad thrashed and screamed, his face bright red from being upside down. I vaulted off and bounded toward him. Squinting up, I noticed he was hanging from his boot. It was stuck on something. A spike nail hung out of the tree, and his boot lace was looped over the nail.

He shrieked uncontrollably, his head hanging a couple feet off the ground. I wrapped my arms around his chest and yelled at him, "Brad, grab onto me!"

Sobbing, he wrapped his arms around my waist.

I lifted him up and shook his leg to get the lace off the nail. Gently turning him upright, I cradled him in my arms. Leaning against the tree, I slid to the ground. Brad grabbed me around the neck and sobbed.

I looked at that nail and giggled. *It's probably the only spike nail sticking out of a tree in 50 miles.* Brad had wandered off the trail again, and as he was riding, he was swinging his legs. He managed to kick the tree and bury the nail under the lace of his boot. The nail pinned his foot to the tree while Seagram kept walking. I'm sure he wiggled and fidgeted trying to get free, just like he'd been doing all week so Seagram didn't think anything of his movements. The nail didn't let go, so Brad was pulled out of the saddle.

Holding him tightly, I said, "If you had been following behind me like I told you, that nail wouldn't have jumped out and grabbed you."

Brad buried his head into my chest. I ruffled his hair. "Now do you know why I wanted you to follow me hoof for hoof?"

Brad sobbed and nodded.

I pulled out my red bandana and wiped the tears from his cheek just as his family came up to see what had happened. They said they'd heard him scream. I smiled up at them. "He'll be fine. He's just learning a little wisdom."

His dad scolded him. "Brad, Rebecca's been telling you all week to follow her. I hope you're going to listen now."

Brad sniffed and nodded.

I hugged Brad and whispered, "A long time ago a friend told me that the definition of wisdom is learning from experience—and it's less painful if it's not your own."

Lord, thank You for reminding me to listen to other people's experiences so that I can acquire wisdom the easy way—by learning from their mistakes. Amen.

16

Buck 'n' Run

Listen to my voice in the morning, Lord.
Each morning I bring my requests to you and wait expectantly.

PSALM 5:3 NLT

The morning sun drifted through my office window, casting shadows across the list of the horses and mules. I was checking off the ones the wranglers would round up and run down to the trailhead for tomorrow's trip. With my pencil I circled the names of 16 mules. *That's easy. That's it for the string. But what am I going to do for horses? We need to buy some more, but it's late in the season. If I buy them now, I'll end up putting a lot of money into hay before I get much use out of them. God, what do you think?* Momentarily I tapped my pencil. *I'd better finish this. The wranglers are waiting.* I drew a line through Melinda. Her whither sore hadn't healed yet. I scratched out Cotton. He'd gotten caught in a fence and peeled some hide off his hind leg. He was still being doctored. Snipe, Star, and Dream all had colts at their sides so I crossed them off.

I drew a big fat X through Amarillo. He was new this year and had a horrible habit of bucking. Just last month D.J. rode him to round up the herd. Amarillo had bucked like a rodeo horse. He dropped his shoulder and then peeled backward so hard that the saddle had come off over his head. It flew through the air with D.J. in it—the breast collar, crupper, and cinch still fastened. Whop! D.J. smashed into the ground, split his head open, and broke his arm. The break was so bad it had to be pinned together at the hospital.

I'm going to ride in to the camp ahead of the guests. I'd rather ride something safe that 14 miles.

I assigned the horses to guests and crew, but when I got to the end of the list I was one horse short. *God, should I buy those horses I looked at last week?* Briefly I doodled. *I don't know if there'll be enough pasture if I do.* I glanced at my watch. Nine thirty. *I'd better get rolling.* Erasing the big fat X, I wrote my name next to Amarillo's.

The next morning a cloud of dust billowed behind the gold pickup as it rattled down the dirt road to the trailhead. I pulled in and hid the truck keys on the shelf in the outhouse. Then I set my slicker, bridle, saddle, saddle blanket, and lunch on the ground next to Amarillo, who was tied to the hitching rack. His copper-colored coat glistened in the sun. Picking up the saddle blanket I said, "You'd better behave today." Amarillo rolled his eyes side to side as I tossed the blanket on his back, followed by the saddle. I cinched it up. After tying my slicker behind the saddle, I stuffed my brown paper lunch sack into one of the saddlebags. I took up the bridle and slipped the bit into Amarillo's mouth. I shook my finger at him. "No bucking. Got it?" He nonchalantly blinked his long, amber eyelashes.

Gathering the reins, I stepped into the saddle and kicked him into a trot. *Trotting the first mile ought to take off some of his steam.* Amarillo's hooves drummed on the hard-packed dirt trail. We floated through the long, flat corridors between the lodgepole pines. Drops of sweat trickled dark streaks down his neck. He smelled hot, so I sat deep in the saddle and drew in the reins to slow him to a walk. The trail wound around the side of a mountain, across a babbling creek, and along a long, flat meadow. The August sun warmed me, and the breeze quietly sighed through the pine boughs. I relaxed in the saddle, watching the forest come to life around me. Squirrels chattered and birds flitted on the breeze.

Suddenly Amarillo exploded. He humped up and jumped straight into the air. My right hand grabbed the saddle horn. With my left I pulled on the reins, hoping to get his head up to stop him from bucking. But mid-air he bowed his neck, tucking his chin by his chest to make it impossible to pull up his head with the reins. His hooves hit the ground with three stiff legs while he bent his right front leg, dropping his shoulder.

The momentum pitched me off balance. I squeezed tight with my legs, trying to pull my body back to center.

Like a cyclone, he pitched and heaved his 1100 pounds in every direction.

My fingernails dug into the saddle.

He threw himself forward, dropping his shoulder again. This time I sailed through the air and landed head first in the dirt.

Amarillo kicked the air with his hind legs. As suddenly as he'd started, he quit. He glanced at me lying in the trail, took a couple steps toward camp, and casually dropped his nose into a patch of green grass.

Moaning, I rolled over and sat up. I wiggled my legs, toes, arms, and fingers. I moved my head. My neck was stiff, but it turned. *Everything seems to work.* I ran my hand through my blond hair and winced. A large knot was growing above my right eye. *No blood—that's good.* My bones creaked as I stood up and brushed off the dust. Scooping up my dusty cowboy hat, I walked toward Amarillo. "Is that grass pretty good?" I asked a bit sarcastically.

He watched me out of the corner of his eye. Keeping his head down and acting as if he hadn't noticed me, he drifted away.

I stopped. "I know what you're doing."

Amarillo paused, keeping his head in the grass. His ears swiveled. He *was* listening.

I took one step forward and stopped.

He watched me as he chomped on grass.

I acted as though I were looking into the sky. Step-by-step I inched closer to him. Just when I could reach out and touch his tail, he moved forward to the next bunch of grass.

I plucked a bunch of green grass and swung wide through the trees, hoping to cut him off and bribe him. But when I got even with him, he bobbed his head as if to say, "Catch me if you can!" Then he trotted away and went over the next hill. I threw the grass at the ground. "You'd better not do this to me the next 11 miles to camp!" I vowed.

I hustled down the trail. I wasn't worried about losing him because he knew where camp was. It was the place where he got grain. He'd definitely pull in there, but I sure wanted to catch him before then! I wanted a horse to ride, *not to walk behind*. I boiled as I hiked down the trail, trying to catch a glimpse of him. Topping a hill I saw a long, brown ribbon in the trail. *A brand-new rein! He'd stepped on it and broken it. That dirty bugger!* I snatched up the piece of leather and trotted down the trail. Rounding the bend, I groaned. Yellowjacket Creek gurgled over rocks. I'd forgotten about it. I took a running jump, landing most of the way over and quickly scampering to shore, my leather boots now sloshing with each step.

Maybe if I cut over the next finger ridge I can come down on the trail in front of Amarillo. I jogged through the tall pines and bushwhacked through snowberry brush. I clawed my way up the steep slope. But when I topped the ridge, Amarillo spotted me and trotted around the bend...and out of sight. Panting, I hiked down to the trail. "If he keeps this up, his name is going to be dog food!"

The next time I saw him was eight miles later...as my boots squished down the trail into camp. He stood under the hay shed, eating grain out of the 55 gallon barrel. He'd pushed aside the lid and had his nose in the feed. Lifting his head out of the barrel, grain and slobber dripped out of his mouth. He looked at me as if saying, "What took you so long?"

It took everything in me to calmly walk up to him. I grabbed the single rein and pulled his head next to mine. "What do you think you're doing? Making *me* walk all the way into camp?" I accused.

The whites showed around his eyes, and he pulled back a little.

"You refused to let me catch you! You only stopped when *you* got what *you* wanted—the grain."

Then deep within I heard, "He's acting just like you."

I gasped. *Me? Have I been acting like Amarillo?* My thoughts drifted to yesterday. When I'd asked God about buying the horses, I'd barely paused for a breath before I was on to the next thing on *my* agenda. I hadn't waited for Him to answer. *Oh Lord, I'm sorry.*

I unsaddled Amarillo and turned him into the pole corral. Walking over to the white canvas wall cook tent, I thought about all the times I'd bucked and run from God. I ducked under the flap and sat on the wooden bench next to the long table. *God, I'm here and I'm listening.* The next hour I forced myself to be quiet. I trained my thoughts on God. He spoke to me through my spirit. I wasn't to buy any more horses until spring. By the time I lit the wood cookstove to start dinner, I knew I'd just learned a priceless lesson—to wait on God.

The rest of that season and through the summer of the next, Amarillo continued to bow his neck and pitch a fit when I least expected it. By fall I was ready to glue a number on him and run him through a livestock sale ring. Somehow he must have known it. He quit acting up. In fact, he never bucked again. Instead he became a topnotch crew horse.

Lord, when my life spins past, remind me to wait and listen to what You have to say. Amen.

17

Lashing Wind

Choose life…that you may love the LORD your God,
that you may obey His voice, and that you may cling to Him,
for He is your life and the length of your days.

DEUTERONOMY 30:20

White billowy clouds quickly rolled through the blue sky as I brushed Amarillo, who was tied to a short and gnarled pine tree. This summer pack trip had brought us to this high-mountain meadow aptly named "Half Moon Park." The small, lush, grassy spot was crescent shaped and seemed suspended like a shelf under the sheer tan rock wall of Scapegoat Mountain, which was part of the Continental Divide. The rim of the cliff above us soared to an elevation of 9200 feet. The opposite edge of the meadow dropped down a steep rocky mountain slope to the valley floor miles below.

I picked up the saddle pad and placed it on Amarillo's back. "Are you ready for a great ride? We're going over the top today." Grabbing the saddle I flipped it onto his back. Tightening the cinch, I looked across the meadow. The wranglers were loading the last mule. The guests stood with their horses, ready to mount and ride the trail.

The wind gusted, tugging at my black cowboy hat. I grabbed it and pulled it down tight. This trip was my first time riding the Divide. I was amazed at how the wind had screamed over the top of the cliff from the time we rode in, two days ago, until now. The clouds looked like they were a part of a movie that was stuck in fast forward. I didn't realize that up here this amount of wind was considered calm. Before the morning was over, I would experience the ruthlessness of the high-country weather patterns—and my life would be changed forever.

While I buckled on my chocolate-brown chaps, suddenly the temperature of the wind dropped several degrees. *That feels like a storm's coming.* I glanced at the blue sky. It was impossible to see what the weather would bring because the storms came in from the west. West was the backside of Scapegoat Mountain. I slipped the bit into Amarillo's mouth and slid the headstall over his ears. The first of the black billowy clouds rolled over the lip of Scapegoat. *That doesn't look good.*

I stepped into the saddle and trotted across the meadow. All the guests had mounted their horses. The crew was busy forming their pack animal strings by tying the mules together. At the far edge of the meadow, Larry, the boss, sat on his bay Arabian gelding. Studying the sky, he zipped up his brown vest. I rode up to him. "What do you think?" I asked.

Larry frowned, "We need to get out of here." He gathered his reins. "I'll lead and have the guys pull string behind me, then you, followed by the guests. There's only a handful of guests. Will you be okay?"

I nodded.

A gust of wind snatched at our hats. Simultaneously we grabbed them and held them tight to our heads until it passed. Larry motioned his arm to the crew. "C'mon, let's roll!" He turned his horse and rode up the trail. Leading the mules, the crew lined out behind him.

Turning in the saddle, I shouted above the wind to the guests, "Follow me." I pulled in behind the last mule. The first quarter mile, the trail ran under the rock wall, which blocked the main force of the wind. I settled into the saddle and studied the trail in front of me. In a hundred yards it narrowed to a two-foot-wide ledge, forming a gray ribbon that seemed to barely cling to a shale rockslide that was littered with boulders. The trail traversed the steep sidehill all the way to the top of the mountain.

Amarillo's hooves soon clattered on the narrow shale trail. The saddle creaked as I turned to see how the guests were doing. The blood drained out of my face. Ominous black clouds blasted over the rock wall. I'd never seen anything like it. The clouds shot in a stream over the cliff, and then rolled in an arc to the floor of the meadow, hammering it. Like an enormous Ferris wheel, the clouds curled backward—sweeping uphill. They crashed into the sheer rock cliff and got sucked up the face and into the clouds blasting the top of Scapegoat. They rolled in a circle over and over again. Faster and faster they mushroomed, seeming to consume the mountain.

A stiff blast of wind hit me. With my right hand I caught my hat and held it to my head. I didn't dare let it go because it might fly in the face of the horse behind me and cause a wreck. The wind bellowed down the rock slide. Another gust slapped me like a two-by-four, momentarily making me lose my balance. With my right hand I grabbed my hat, with my left the reins and saddle horn. I leaned into the wind.

The gale rumbled around the mountain like a freight train. Like an invisible wall, a blast buffeted us with so much power it pushed Amarillo sideways a few inches. I gasped. Amarillo stopped. The wind was deafening as it roared past my ears and beat my batwing chaps against my legs.

Breathlessly, I looked down my left stirrup. Just inches to the left of Amarillo's hooves was the edge of the cliff. *If the wind gusts again, we're going over,* I thought. *And shale is flat and smooth on top. It's worse than walking on ice. If we get blown off, Amarillo won't be able to get his footing.* I shuddered. *He'll probably break a leg while he struggles to stand. And I might fall underneath his feet and get trampled.* I held my breath as I reined and urged him to the uphill side of the trail.

Still hanging on to my hat, I tucked my head and glanced back at the guests. Their eyes were squinted against the wind and their faces were tense with fear. With white knuckles I clung to the saddle horn. *How much stronger can the wind blow? What if it sweeps me out of the saddle and throws me into the sky like a rag doll?* I focused on the mule in front of me.

Another wall of wind collided against us. The mule in front of me braced itself as it skidded sideways, knocking rocks off the edge of the trail. I watched them bounce down the cliff and out of sight.

Another blast pounded us. In horror I felt the gust shove Amarillo toward the edge. My heart pounded. *If the storm picks me up, how high will it toss me before I plummet to the ground?*

The black mushrooming clouds swallowed us, blocking the sun, making it as dark as twilight. The storm whipped us with dust and pebbles. Even the mountain rumbled and quaked under the force.

Amarillo dug his hooves into the shale, trying to hold himself on the narrow ledge.

Holding my breath, I squinted, still clutching the saddle horn. The wind's icy fingers pried at me. I knew it wanted to pluck me out of the saddle. I squeezed my legs tight, gripping the saddle, and leaned into the wind. Terror filled me as I watched Amarillo's hooves dance close to the edge again. *God, what do I do?* I pleaded. *Help us.*

My horse's hooves slid another inch. He braced against the wind.

He can't stay on the trail with me sitting in the saddle. I'm creating too much wind resistance. Holding the reins and my hat in my left hand, I slowly put my weight in the right stirrup, the side by the wall.

Amarillo skidded to the edge. Rocks tumbled off and disappeared.

I held my breath.

Quickly I slipped my leg over the saddle and swung to the ground. I lifted my leg to take a step, but the wind fluttered my chaps hard and grabbed my leg. With all my might I pushed my leg to the trail and dug my leather boot into the shale. *Maybe I should shed the chaps?* But I knew if I took them off the wind would snatch them away like a kite and send them sailing—maybe into the horses and mules behind me. That would scare them half to death, and they might stampede off the cliff. *I've got to leave them on.*

I glanced back at Amarillo. He shouldered into the wind and moved to the center of the trail. I leaned into the wind. With my left hand I held my hat to my head, with my right I held the reins. I took a small step forward and dug in my toes. Mid-step the wind buffeted me, shoving me off balance. I crouched lower, but my 135 pounds was nothing compared to the ruthless wind. For my next step, I didn't lift my foot off the ground. Instead I skidded it forward. *That's better.* I glanced back at my horse. The wind didn't seem to be thrusting him sideways as much. I looked back at the guests. They too had dismounted.

Black clouds boiled around us as we picked our way through the boulder-strewn trail. One grueling step at a time the mules advanced. Their packs created so much wind resistance they swayed back and forth. They'd take one step forward and the wind would pound them, so they'd put one foot to the side to catch their balance. Callously it tossed them around the trail. A couple times it looked as if the wind momentarily lifted them off their feet. *What if the wind picks them up and tosses them down the mountain?* I begged, *God, please do something!*

The closer we got to the top of Scapegoat, the more violent the wind became. My ears throbbed from its deafening roar. We were lost in the dark and wicked inner sanctum of the storm. It churned, pushing and pulling us every direction. Then the black clouds vomited hail. Ice marbles were strewn at us from every direction, beating down on us.

Suddenly a gust grabbed my batwing chaps and pulled me off my feet. My shoulder slammed the ground. I clawed the trail, my fingers clutching at loose stones. Then I saw a boulder up ahead. Using all my strength, I heaved my body up and toward the huge rock. I reached it and gratefully wrapped my arms around it. Clinging to it, my mind whirled. *Thank You, God, for this rock!*

My fingernails dug into the indentations of the boulder. I forced my thoughts on God. *God, You are my rock…You are my salvation…In You I shall trust.* Strength flowed through my spirit. *You are my rock. You are my salvation. In You I shall trust.* The more I focused on His Word, the bolder my thoughts. *You are my deliverer. You will get us safely off this mountain. You are almighty. You are all-powerful.* I felt something nudging my back. I turned and looked into Amarillo's muzzle. His soft brown eyes looked at me questioningly. Tears flowed down my cheeks; the wind swept them away. Corralling my emotions, I forced my thoughts back to God. *You, God, are more powerful than this storm. We will get off this mountain. Help me be strong for the guests.*

I looked down the trail. Although the wind buffeted the guests, they were still standing. Slowly they picked their way. *I'm glad that each of them has at least 50 pounds on me, and none of them are wearing chaps.* Ten feet up the trail was another boulder. *Okay, Rebecca, you've got to move.* I scanned the trail. Pulling my feet underneath me, I crouched. *God, You hung the stars in place. You hold the winds in Your hands. I know You love me. I'm trusting You to tell me when to move.*

Focusing on the next boulder, I waited. Suddenly in my spirit I heard, "Move!"

Adrenaline rushed through me. I pushed off from the rock, still holding the reins. Staying low to lessen the wind resistance, I shuffled forward, digging one boot into the shale, and then the other. Behind me Amarillo carefully picked his way. *Only one more step,* I repeated over and over. Once again I dug in my boots and wrapped my arms around a boulder. *Okay, God, we did it. I need You to help me again.*

A torrent of wind howled down the rockslide, whipping the hail away but blasting small stones at us. With white knuckles I hung on to the boulder. I squinted and held my breath, not wanting to inhale dirt. The next boulder was about eight feet away. I waited. *God, You are my strong tower. You are my fortress. You are my shield.*

Once again from within I heard, "Move!"

Up the trail I went, capturing one boulder at a time as God urged me forward. Gradually the wind eased. By the time we topped Scapegoat

Mountain, the brunt of the storm had passed. Although the wind still howled, it now sounded like a whisper. I stepped to the side of Amarillo. "Good job, buddy." I swung into the saddle and waited for the guests to arrive and mount up.

I was numb and in shock. I rode down the steep trail that wound through the pines. My mind churned. *What happened back there?* At the beginning of the storm I begged and pleaded with God to do something. I was scared out of my mind. I didn't know what to do. The wind was powerful enough to sweep me away. I felt totally helpless. But while I clung to the first boulder, a new understanding about God flowed through my spirit. He didn't want me to beg and plead. He loved me. All He wanted from me was to have faith in Him, in His power, in His ability, and in His love for me. As I lost focus on my circumstances and tightened my mind on who He is, His strength flowed through me. When I firmly stood on His Word, He gave me the strength to survive and persevere.

Sitting around the campfire that night, all of us shared our personal battles of weathering the storm. For me, clinging to the boulder gave me a nugget of faith I will carry with me the rest of my life.

I'm in awe of Your mighty power, Lord. Thank You for giving me the opportunity to build my faith on You—my rock. Amen.

18

Hobbling Along

Suppose one of you has a hundred sheep and loses one of them.
Does he not leave the ninety-nine in the open country
and go after the lost sheep until he finds it?

LUKE 15:4

The wispy morning fog floated between the green tents, down the long meadow, and into the pines. The blue-green kitchen tarp was pitched on a bank above Basin Creek, which gurgled over rocks as it flowed past. Opening the woodstove's door, I placed a small log on the fire and closed it. Immediately the stove chugged smoke. The blue enamelware coffeepot belched steam. Lifting the lid, I added the coffee. The grounds boiled and churned. *Just like the inside of me,* I thought.

Richard, one of the guests, strolled over to the woodstove holding a yellow coffee cup. He ran his hand through his black hair and yawned.

I glanced at him. "Sleep well?"

He nodded. On the notepad next to the stove he scribbled, "Two eggs—over easy, bacon, three pancakes." He held out his cup. I poured the coffee. Richard nodded thanks and walked through the meadow to the morning campfire that was blazing a couple feet high.

Placing the griddle on the stove, I laid out bacon to fry. One by one the guests filtered through the kitchen, wrote down their breakfast orders, filled their coffee cups, and wandered to the fire. I looked longingly at the inviting flames and the camaraderie. People sat in camp chairs while warming their hands, laughing, and sipping coffee. I sighed and wrestled with my emotions. *As long as they get their coffee, they're happy.* I flipped a piece of bacon. *That's not a nice thought.* I watched it sizzle and curl. *Lord, some days I feel so…unnoticed…unappreciated… so invisible. And to top it off, today I have to do double-duty.*

Normally at daybreak the wranglers rounded up the herd that had been turned loose to graze. They'd haze the horses and mules through the meadow, the bell on the lead horse ringing da-ding, da-ding, da-ding. That was the guests' wakeup call. After pushing them into the rope corral and saddling them, the cowboys would hustle to the kitchen and pull a campstool next to the cookstove. Holding out their cups for a shot of "cowboy black gold," they'd tell stories of the previous night's wrangling adventures.

But not this morning. Instead, after they'd saddled the animals, they rode their horses through the tall wet grass up to the kitchen tarp. They tipped their cowboy hats and said, "Asher's missing. We're going to look for him." Spinning their horses, they cantered out of the meadow.

Today was a moving day on our summer pack trip, which meant the crew would tear down the entire camp, pack everything onto the mules, ride to the next campsite 18 miles down the trail, and set the whole thing back up again. Because the wranglers had ridden out of camp, I'd be cooking, washing dishes, and packing the kitchen. Plus there would only be the boss and me to tear down the camp and mantie on the loads. I glanced at the campfire. *As long as the work gets done, I bet nobody notices…or cares. I just kind of float in the background.*

I reached under the kitchen table, slid out the cardboard box filled with groceries, and carried it to a mantie tarp that was lying on the ground a few feet from the kitchen. It was the signal that the box was ready to be wrapped in canvas. I stacked the second grocery box on top of the first and glanced at my watch. The wranglers had been gone an hour. *What's taking them so long? I hope Asher's okay.* My heart raced. *Why did we put hobbles on him last night?* Asher, a young, rawboned, sorrel mule with a roach-clipped salt-and-pepper-colored mane, was new to the outfit this season. He didn't have much in the way of training. This was his first summer trip, and the last couple days he'd been a bugger to catch. When we pushed the herd into the rope corral, Asher would filter in with the others. But when it came time to catch him, he'd duck under the rope and escape. It took four people to catch him in the rope corral, three on the outside to keep him from ducking the rope, and one on the inside pushing him into a corner.

Because Asher was so hard to catch, the wranglers had decided to hobble him last night. They'd buckled the wide leather straps below each of Asher's front ankles. The heavy-duty, seven-inch chain that runs between the two straps was supposed to keep him from stretching his legs into a trot or run, making him easier to catch. But now the mule was missing. My mind raced. *What's happened to him?*

I went back into the kitchen. The pancake batter sizzled as I poured some onto the griddle. *What if his hobbles got hung up on a log or tangled in the brush? How will we ever find him?* The next half hour I called the guests' names and handed them plates stacked high with pancakes, eggs, and bacon. They grabbed their food and immediately drifted back to the campfire. Finally I heard the sound of pounding hooves on the hard-packed dirt trail. My excitement quickly faded. They weren't leading Asher. With drawn faces, the wranglers reined their horses over to me.

I walked to the edge of the kitchen tarp. "Why don't you go tie up. You'd better get some food in your bellies. It's going to be a long day."

While the wranglers shoveled down syrup-drenched pancakes, Larry, the boss, picked up a stick. Drawing an outline of the meadow in the dirt, he said, "We'll split up." With the stick, he tapped the east side of the meadow. "I want you two to search over here," he said, pointing to two cowboys. They nodded. Larry tapped the stick on the west side. "I'll take this area. And Rebecca, I want you to ride this side. If you don't find anything, meet back here in an hour."

I turned, rolled my eyes, and carried a stack of dirty dishes to the table. *Now it's triple duty!*

Tossing my saddle on Amarillo, I swung up and headed out. I cast to-and-fro along the riverbank. How do you look for a mule in thick willow brush when you can't see 10 feet in front of your face? What if Asher got tangled up and fell down? How would I see him if he's lying on the ground? Amarillo's hooves clattered on the pebbles of a wide creek bed. It was impossible to see tracks in the rocks. I squeezed my legs and urged Amarillo through a thick patch of willows. Reaching up and pushing the tall brush out of my face, I listened for movement. A few songbirds greeted the day and a squirrel chattered from the pines, and that was it. The next hour I combed the riverbed and the adjoining meadow. Nothing. I turned Amarillo toward camp.

The horses and mules stood tied inside the rope corral, switching their tails at the flies. Larry and the wranglers squatted on their boots, gathered around a map that lay on the ground, weighted down with a rock on each corner. I guided Amarillo toward them. "Nothing, huh?" I asked. They all shook their heads.

My saddle creaked as I stepped down. "I didn't even see a track."

Larry studied the map. "He's got to be here somewhere...unless he left the country. If he did, he'll head back to the trailhead and be standing at the corrals when we get out." Larry shook his head. "But it's not likely that a mule will head out by himself."

The blazing sun was straight overhead by now. Sweat trickled down my neck. I shook my head. *We haven't gotten packed up yet. It's going to be an all-nighter if we don't find him pretty soon.* I sat on my heels in the grass and looked at the map. *Lord, where is he? How do we find him?*

Larry rubbed the corners of his brown moustache. He pointed to a thin strip of meadow on the map. "This is an out-of-the-way spot. The horses usually don't go in here, but let's line out and sweep through."

Saddles groaned as we swung up. Spreading out about 100 feet apart, we rode side-by-side, combing through waist-deep grass that swayed in the breeze. I studied every dip, looking for an ear or some kind of movement. *Lord, he's only one mule, and yes, we've got a bunch back at camp. But we need to find him. He's important. Show us where he is.* The horses' hooves clattered over the pebbles, through the willows, and across the creek. In the meadow on the other side of the creek, we swept through a stand of pines toward the base of the mountain. Suddenly Amarillo's ears perked up. We topped a small brushy knob and looked down into the grassy gully. There stood that sorrel mule, munching grass. His head came up, grass hanging out of the corners of his mouth. He looked at us as if saying, "What took you so long?" I giggled with relief. The chain of Asher's hobbles was tangled around a fallen log and he couldn't move, so he just stood and ate while he patiently waited for rescue.

The wranglers haltered him and unbuckled his hobbles. We drifted back to camp. I fell in behind the errant mule. *Thank You, Lord, for helping us find Asher.* When we rode into the meadow where camp was set up, a chorus of whinnies and brays greeted us from the rope corral. I glanced at my watch: noon. *The corral is brimming with horses and mules, and we spent all these hours searching for just one. But we wouldn't have left without him. We needed him to pack loads.* Then I had a strange thought. *When Asher buckled down and did his work, I never paid any attention to him. It was like he was invisible because he was part of the team of horses and mules. I didn't think of them separately—only as a unit.* My thoughts continued. *Kind of like me. Even though I feel unappreciated and invisible, my feelings are not reflecting the truth. The truth is that I'm a valuable part of the team.*

We rode toward the campfire. It popped and cracked as Richard threw on another log. The guests cheered and clapped when they glimpsed Asher. The rest of the morning spun past as we tore down camp, packed the mules, and rode down the trail.

We arrived with just enough daylight to set up camp in the Dana-her Valley and eat dinner. Twilight glimmered in the sky as I dried the last plate and closed the kitchen boxes for the night. The next morning when the guests filtered to the campfire, the nagging feeling of being unappreciated returned. But this time I turned it around. I kept repeating to myself, *I'm* not *invisible and unappreciated; I'm part of an awesome team.* And each morning it grew easier to chase the negative thoughts away.

My greatest reward was when we stood in the airport, saying goodbye to the guests. Richard turned to me and said, "Rebecca, thank you for the wonderful trip. It was the first time in years we were able to sit back and relax. We knew the crew had everything handled."

Lord, help me to quit focusing on myself. Instead, please remind me that I'm an important part of Your team. Amen.

19

Boots to Boxes

Your heavenly Father knows that you need
[food to eat, something to drink, and clothes to wear].
But seek first his kingdom and his righteousness,
and all these things will be given to you as well.

MATTHEW 6:33

The battery-powered alarm clock beeped. When I reached for it, the cold mountain air rushed into my sleeping bag. I hit the snooze bar. The numbers glowed. It was five o'clock. I burrowed into the warmth of the bag and then bolted up. *Five o'clock! I've got to get going!* My tent was pitched in the Danaher Valley, 24 miles into the heart of the Bob Marshall Wilderness Complex. By seven tonight I planned on being at a business meeting in the heart of Portland, Oregon. I had timed everything to the second. I would cook breakfast for the 15 of us, tear down and pack the kitchen, ride 24 miles to the trailhead, drive 45 minutes to the ranch, shower, grab my suitcase, drive an hour-and-a-half to the Missoula airport, fly to Portland, catch a taxi to my hotel, and walk to the convention center—all in 14 hours. I'd be pushing my horse and myself to the limit. *Can I do it?*

My mind raced as I slipped into my jeans and shirt. I rolled up my sleeping pad and stuffed my sleeping bag. I glanced at the clock: 5:17. No time to read my Bible. I squashed down my duffel, placed the Bible inside, and zipped it closed. My heart felt sick. *Maybe I'll have time to read after I light the cookstove and start the coffee.* I pulled out the Bible, zipped the bag again, and tossed my stuff out the tent door. Within minutes I tore down the tent, tossed my gear on the pile to be packed on the mules, and ran to the kitchen tarp.

Setting the Bible and the alarm clock on the kitchen box where I could keep an eye on the time, I fired up the woodstove and set up the coffee. I raced to the creek three times with five-gallon metal buckets, dipping them into the water and hauling out our morning water supply. Pausing, I glanced at the clock: 5:46. The jingling of the bell on the lead horse drifted across the meadow as the wranglers pushed the herd into the rope corral. Bacon spattered on the cast iron griddle as I scurried to lay out the makings for the needed sack lunches.

At 6:14, Bill, my boss, strolled in from the corral. He stroked his dark moustache as he watched me frantically prepare breakfast. "So you think you're going to make it out of here on time?"

"I've got it all planned."

Bill shook his head as I poured him a steaming cup of coffee. The wranglers drifted under the kitchen tarp and set camp chairs next to the woodstove, where they warmed their hands. I moved my Bible out of the way and asked, "Okay, what do you guys want for your lunches?"

Now it was 6:30. The guests drifted over to the cookstove. I flipped hotcakes, fried eggs, and poured coffee until I squeezed in a moment to shovel down an egg myself. By 7:30 I had fed all 15 of us. Frantically I scrubbed dishes and packed them into the kitchen boxes. Eight o'clock. I packed my Bible in the kitchen box and fastened the latch. My stomach turned over. *Maybe I'll have time at the ranch.* I opened the box and pulled out the Bible.

I turned around to see Bill leading Britt, my palomino, toward me.

Handing me the reins he said, "I hope you don't mind that I saddled him. You'd better ride."

I said thank you, gave all the guests hugs, stuffed my Bible into a saddlebag, and swung a leg over the saddle. Tightening down my black hat, I kicked Britt into his running walk. The next intense 4 hours and 24 miles disappeared in a cloud of dust from his flying feet. When the trail narrowed and rimmed the edge of a cliff, I slowed Britt and pondered my long-term priorities—a truck and a new horse trailer were on the top of the list. As soon as the trail widened and flattened out, I kicked Britt into his "boogying" gear.

At noon I topped a hill and headed down to the trailhead. Going into the corral I stripped off the saddle and turned Britt loose. I remembered the Bible. I dug through my saddlebags, pulled it out, and tossed it onto the seat of the truck. I threw my gear into the back of the pickup. A cloud of dust swirled behind me as I zoomed to the ranch, where I showered and traded my boots for heels and my chaps for a dress. Tossing my Bible into my suitcase, I thought, *Maybe tonight.* Then I screeched out of the ranch and headed for the airport.

I plastered my face to the plane's window as I descended into Portland. I caught my breath. After two months of working in the wilderness and then my quick trip here, I wasn't prepared for the sight. Buildings stacked next to buildings, cars and buses jamming the freeways—all those boxes. Tall boxes. Small boxes. Medium boxes. Below me lay nothing but boxes. I heard a lady in front of me say, "Oh, look at that beautiful home." *Just a fancy box,* I thought.

When we deplaned, people at the airport rushed to their next boxes. While waiting for a taxi, I heard kids marveling at the sleek boxes that drove past.

I took a yellow box to my hotel, where they assigned me my very own box. I took a moving box up to my personal box and tossed my cloth box full of clothes onto the springy box I'd sleep on. I tossed my clothes into a wooden box, went into the ceramic tile box to touch-up my makeup, which was packaged in colorful boxes. I sprinted over to the meeting center, a huge open box. All night long speakers talked about all the cars (fast boxes) and homes (pretty boxes) they'd worked so hard to achieve.

After the meeting I went back to the large box, went to my personal box, and flopped down on the springy box. Boxy thoughts scurried through my head. Thoughts of spending my life working to get more boxes, faster boxes, and bigger boxes. One thing all the boxes had in common? They were all hollow. All the boxes I had accumulated through my life will mean nothing when the lid on my last box is closed and I'm placed in the ground.

I fluffed the soft, oblong box my head lay on and reviewed my day. From the time I woke up in the Danaher Valley until now, all my goals were about achieving boxes—or rushing to the next box. Not one of my priorities would have a lasting impact on anything or anybody. I'd planned my day down to the second, but I hadn't scheduled any time for God. I had stacked all my boxes first. *It's time to change that.*

The next morning I set my alarm a half hour early so I would have time to read the Bible and pray. Over the next few weeks I set spiritual goals, such as how much time I would invest into building my faith by reading and praying daily and who I wanted to share my faith with. These were eternal priorities.

Sure I still have box goals, but my relationship with God has become my priority.

> *Lord, remind me to keep my eyes off the boxes that distract me and show me how to push myself to the limit for You. Amen.*

20

Stuck Together

Watch your tongue and keep your mouth shut,
and you will stay out of trouble.

PROVERBS 21:23 NLT

Two horses and nine sweaty mules loaded with packs stood tied to the hitching rail. The hot sun beat down on them. As usual, the horseflies were droning and circling, annoying them. Bob and I had helped the guests saddle up at the trailhead. They would take a meandering route to enjoy the horses and scenery, while we loaded the mules and rode straight to camp.

Bob and I arrived at the six white canvas tents, a tack shed, and a rickety wooden outhouse that made up the little village we called Monture Creek Camp. We were going to spend five days here fishing and horseback riding.

I untied a big sorrel mule named Roman because of his prominent nose. I led him over to the cook tent where Bob was untying the sling rope from a load on a black mule. I asked, "Are you ready for another round of guests?"

Bob grunted as he lifted the hundred-pound pack off the mule and set it on the ground. "I'm ready for hunting season. But they looked like nice folks."

I twisted Roman's lead rope and under my breath I said, "Yeah, all except for that doctor. Can you believe he said he was an 'experienced rider'? When I helped fit his saddle, he had no idea how to mount. And then he argued with me about the length of the stirrups. He wanted to ride like a jockey. His knees would have been thrashed by the time he rode the four hours here. He's going to be a pain."

Bob rested his hand on the black mule's rump as he walked to the other side. Untying the sling rope he said, "And I was looking forward to a great last trip for the summer. I'll stay away from him."

Reaching into my pocket I pulled out a Jolly Rancher hard candy. "Do you want one?" I offered.

As Bob shook his head, Roman whiffed the apple-flavored candy. He stretched his lips for it. I tapped his nose. "You, Mr. Roman, are a mule. And mules don't get candy. It's bad for your teeth."

Roman wiggled his lips and bobbed his head.

I giggled. "How do you know you'd like it?" I asked.

Nuzzling my hand, he looked at me and batted his long, red eyelashes.

Slipping off the crinkly plastic wrapper I said, "Okay, but you'd better not waste a perfectly good Jolly Rancher." Roman gently picked the candy out of the palm of my hand with his lips. He rolled it around in his mouth. It clacked against his teeth. His eyes widened. I'm sure he'd never tasted anything with such a big burst of flavor. He smacked his lips and drooled.

Bob and I both smiled.

Roman rolled the Jolly Rancher between his teeth and then bit down. I looked at him with dismay. When I did that the candy would hold my teeth together.

Sure enough, Roman's teeth did the same thing. Drool dripped out his lips as he wrinkled his nose and turned his head sideways, trying to unclench his teeth. The Jolly Rancher held fast. He tried grinding his teeth from side to side but that didn't work. Then he rubbed his mouth on his leg. It didn't matter what he did, he couldn't get his teeth unstuck.

Hooves clattered on the trail and voices drifted through the pines. The guests rode into view. Bob screwed down his cowboy hat and asked, "Which one's the doctor?"

Roman twisted his jaw, his mouth still clamped shut.

Insight flooded my mind. I suddenly realized that's what I should have done. Shaking my head I said, "Bob, I should have kept my mouth shut. I was so frustrated with that guy, but I never should have vented and said anything bad about him."

Hoofbeats drummed behind me. I turned and looked into the smiling face of the doctor. He wiggled his legs in the stirrups and said, "Rebecca, I want to thank you for telling me about riding with longer stirrups. About halfway down the trail we stopped and made them even longer."

I grinned, glanced at Bob, and then looked back at the rider. "You're welcome. It's going to be a fun trip."

Lord, help me hold my tongue. If I feel a need to vent, remind me to keep it between You and me. Amen.

21

Leaky Slicker

Stop being bitter and angry and mad at others.
Don't yell at one another or curse each other or ever be rude.
Instead, be kind and merciful, and forgive others,
just as God forgave you because of Christ.

EPHESIANS 4:31-32 CEV

The brisk October breeze gently sang through the pines and the sun warmed my back. I unzipped my winter jacket a few inches and loosened my wool scarf. Cotton-ball clouds floated over the mountain peaks. Brilliant-gold aspen leaves lazily spiraled to the forest floor. I leaned forward in the saddle, squeezed my knees, and clucked to my bay gelding to move into a trot. I was by myself and on the way to the hunting camp 24 miles away. On a good day, if Czar and I moved at a good clip with no stops, it would take us seven hours. The hunters and guides had packed in a couple days ago, but I hadn't because of a commitment in civilization. Today I was swapping out with Karen, my boss, who had stood in as cook for me.

It was a perfect day. I wasn't pulling a pack string of mules. I didn't have to watch out for guests or crew. And camp was already set up.

When I'd ride in tonight, the lanterns would be glowing inside the canvas tents and dinner would be warming on the woodstove.

Well…it would have been a perfect day except for my encounter this morning with Becky. Boy, she could irritate me. We were opposites. I was a tall beanpole. She was short and rather stout. I fit with the crew like a glove, but she seemed standoffish. I loved working in the woods and disliked returning to civilization. Becky didn't come into the hills. She cooked at the ranch and managed the lodge and cabins while the rest of us were on trips.

Becky's job was enormous. It took an incredibly organized person to iron out the details of meals, groceries, lodging, and vehicles at the trailheads and coordinate the constant comings and goings of guests and crews. In the summer there were two crews, and in the fall there were three.

I frowned as I rocked in the saddle and thought about all the things Becky forgot to pack for my trips. The worst part was that once we rode into the wilderness, there wasn't any place to get supplies. It wasn't uncommon for me to be short one steak, which meant *I* went without any meat for dinner. Or I might discover that the specific food items I'd requested, such as cheese and crackers for mid-afternoon snacks, were never purchased. I hadn't heard of anything missing on the other trips. By mid-summer I wondered if she was shorting supplies for my trips on purpose.

Czar's hooves clattered on rocks. I slowed him to a walk as we climbed up Whiskey Ridge. When it leveled out on the top, I zipped up my winter jacket. The temperature dropped at least 10 degrees, and the breeze had changed directions. *Not good. It's out of the north,* I thought. Ominous dark-gray clouds marched over the pine-studded mountain. *Good thing I bought that waterproof slicker that will fit over my winter jacket. This could turn nasty.* The black clouds spit a few raindrops. Untying the dark-green raincoat from its place on the back of the saddle, I shrugged it on and then pushed Czar into a mile-eating walk. By the time I dropped off Whiskey Ridge into the Dry Fork, the breeze had given way to a side wind that pelted us with sleet and snow. Pulling up my collar, I tipped my head down, so the bill on my wool "Elmer Fudd hat" would keep the snow out of my eyes. It had flaps that came down over my ears, and I was grateful for the warmth. The wind bit my face. Czar squinted his eyes and bowed his neck. He picked his way down the trail that wound through the knee-high wet grass.

The wind bellowed through the full-length of the valley and blasted into us. Czar braced against it. By the time we reached the north end of the valley, daylight was fading and snow had built up on the shoulders of my slicker. Then I felt a cold drop on my shoulder. *What?* Quickly I whisked off the snow. Unzipping my slicker I looked at a dark and wet spot engulfing the top of my winter jacket. *This raincoat is supposed to be waterproof!* The slicker had obviously been leaking for quite a while, but I hadn't felt it because it had to soak through my winter jacket, down vest, wool sweater, turtleneck, and long johns top before hitting my skin. An alarm sounded through my mind: "Never, never, *never* get wet in the wilderness during a storm."

One of the biggest threats to living in the woods was not the animals or encounters with people—it was hypothermia, when a person's core body temperature drops from its usual 98.6 degrees to 95 degrees or lower. And when a person's clothing gets wet, it draws body heat out. Hypothermia creeps in slowly, clouding a person's thoughts. Over the years I'd drilled the symptoms into my head: hunger, shivering, blueness of skin, loss of coordination starting with fingers and then advancing to stumbling. Judgment is gradually impaired, and during the final stages can lead to amnesia, apathy, and drowsiness. In the last stages, the violent shivering stops. At the end, all the person wants to do is to lie down and sleep. Death follows.

The wind gusted. I hunkered in the saddle, the snow pelting my numb face. My thoughts whirled. *I still have a couple hours to ride. There's not a shelter where I can build a fire to dry out.* I pulled the scarf higher on my neck. *This storm feels like it's going to get worse. If I stop, the snow could pile up and strand me out here.* I leaned forward and patted Czar's neck. "Let's boogie." He quickened his pace.

Over the next couple miles the temperature plummeted. The snow fell so thickly I could only see 20 feet in front of me. Constantly I brushed the snow off my shoulders, but the wetness seeped through. My upper body became damp. Shivering, I unbuckled my saddlebags and pulled out one of the two sandwiches Becky had packed for me. I peeled back the plastic bag and took a bite. *Turkey—yuck! Becky knows that turkey is on the bottom of my like list.* I was so hungry I polished off both sandwiches. In my mind I notched another offense against her.

A mile later I felt cold and clammy. Reining in Czar, I slipped out of the saddle. *I'd better walk a ways to warm up.* With Czar trailing me, I slogged down the trail. Earlier in the day rain had poured, creating ruts in the trail that had filled with water. The blizzard had then filled them with snow, forming deep slush. I shoved my clunky winter boots through the mess while my mind replayed the situations where I felt Becky had offended me. In a mile I was exhausted, but my body had warmed up a bit. I climbed back into the saddle. Over the next couple miles I would walk until I warmed up and then ride to gather back my strength. By now I was so wet and cold that my teeth chattered even when I was walking.

The wind howled and snow drifted across the valley. Darkness swallowed us as the sun set behind the mountains and clouds blocked the moon. Only the snow glowed faintly. Pine trees moaned, objecting to the force of the wind twisting their limbs. Violently shivering in the saddle, I opened and closed my hands trying to warm them. The temperature kept plunging, turning the trail into a sheet of ice. Mile after mile I hunkered in the saddle against the wind. My bones ached from the cold. It felt like my inner heater had switched off. A gust of wind thundered down the valley and collided with us, pushing us sideways. Czar's metal shoes glided on the ice. He wobbled and locked his knees, trying to stand. I grabbed his mane. "Easy boy," I comforted. The wind swept my words away. Czar carefully inched his feet across the ice. I slumped in the saddle and shook my head, trying to clear it.

How far to camp? Sheets of ice entombed me. Disoriented, I squinted into the black storm that pelted us with snow. *Where are we?*

A tree snapped, broken by the wind. It crashed to the ground, and Czar jumped. He shuffled one of his front feet forward. Just as he put his weight on it, he skidded. The leg buckled. I tipped forward, grabbing his mane. My shifting weight pushed him off-center again. His feet slipped on the ice. Catching himself, he stopped and stood with all four feet firmly planted. I breathed a sigh of relief and slipped out of the saddle to walk a while.

I took a couple steps. My foot slipped out from underneath me. Falling on my side, I curled into a ball. *It feels so good to lie down,* I thought. A warning bell clanged and my mind said, "Get up! Get up!" Exhausted I pulled myself to my feet and stood weaving, my thoughts groggy. I blinked. The stormy night consumed me. I stood still until Czar nudged me forward with his nose. I took a deep breath. *I can do this.* I forced myself to put one foot forward. "Just one more step," I told myself over and over.

I shuffled along the icy trail for what seemed an eternity. The wind blasted my face. Snowflakes stuck to my eyelashes. I had to hold my eyelids partially closed because my contacts kept freezing. The trail dipped down a small hill to a river. I stopped, my mind muddled. *Danaher River?* I stepped next to Czar. His body was crusted with snow. My body felt so heavy, that I leaned against him before heaving myself into the saddle. I urged him forward. He stepped over the edge of the bank and stopped at the ice that extended four feet into the river. The beaver dams had caused the river to back up. With little flow, a thick layer of ice had formed at this crossing. I knew we'd fall though the ice after a few steps but the river was only three feet deep here. And the bottom consisted of pebbles, so it would be fairly easy to walk on. Czar knew we'd fall through too. His instincts shouted to him that the ice was dangerous and that he might fall through and drown.

I squeezed my knees, telling him to go forward. He backed up. Exhausted, I thumped his side. But kick as I may, he refused to step onto the ice. My hands felt like clubs. I fumbled with the reins and switched him. He whirled around. I turned him back. He walked to the edge but refused to go further. My speech had grown thick. "Czar, cross!" He stood frozen like a block of ice. A thought whispered from the back of my foggy brain: *Ride to the high crossing.* I turned Czar north as my thoughts battled each other. *The high crossing would add 45 minutes to this agonizing trip.*

The wind gusted and swirled. I quit shivering and drooped in the saddle. The black night and the rocking motion from Czar's stride lulled me. "If only I could lie down and sleep for a while" kept circling in my thoughts. My body wasn't part of me anymore. I couldn't feel my hands. I shook my head to wake up. From the depths of my mind a thought slowly drifted forward: *Tie the reins together before you drop them.* I could barely fumble a knot. I let the reins fall on Czar's neck as my hands dropped to my lap.

I squinted but couldn't make out any shapes. Nothing felt familiar. *Are we going the right way? Should we go the other direction?* A red flag waved in my mind. "Let Czar lead" floated through the haze. The wind whipped us. I slouched deeper in the saddle, my mind bogged down. Czar's hooves clattered over pebbles and then splashed through water. He climbed up the hill and wove through the pines that finally broke the force of the wind, providing some relief. With each step, his hooves creaked through the cold snow. Suddenly his head popped up. He whinnied. I shook my head to clear the fuzziness. I heard answering whinnies. I squinted. In the distance three Coleman gas lanterns glowed from what were probably the hitching rack and corrals. The lanterns cut through the fog of my mind. I sighed and thumped Czar with my frozen hand. "Good boy," I whispered.

My boss, Jack, and the wranglers heard the horses neighing. They came out from the tents and stood under the lanterns waiting for me at the corral. Czar finally got to them. Jack walked over and frowned at my iced-over jacket and blue lips. "We were just getting ready to send a search party."

My tongue was thick as I slurred out, "Czar wouldn't cross on the ice by the beaver dams. We took the high crossing."

He shook his head. "We never would have looked for you up there." Reaching out his hand, Jack helped me out of the saddle. He turned to the cowboys and said, "Unsaddle Czar and grain him." Then he walked with me to my tent. "The guys lit a fire in your woodstove a couple of hours ago. It's toasty warm in there."

Jack held open the flap. Heat boiled out. Uncomfortably he shifted his weight and looked into my eyes. A tone of worry sounded in his voice when he asked, "Will you be okay getting changed into dry clothes?"

I nodded.

"Right after you get changed, I want you to come to the cook tent."

I nodded my head again and stepped next to the woodstove.

Chunks of ice fell off my jacket as I held my hands close to the stove. They felt like they were on fire, so I stepped back. Gradually my mind thawed. I glanced at my watch. It had taken Czar and me more than nine hours to get to camp.

After a few minutes I could open and close my hands. I'd surely been in the final stages of hypothermia. If it hadn't been for God's warning bells going off in my head and for Czar, I'd probably be lying frozen on the trail.

Slowly the heat penetrated my body. Sitting on the edge of my hay bed, I changed clothes and frowned as I pulled off my wool pants. The hem was crusted with mud from walking through the slop on the trail. *I'll have to send these out with the next pack string for Becky to wash.* I groaned. *I wonder if she'll put them in the dryer and shrink them.*

I hesitated. *Becky's not even here and I'm complaining about her.* Normally when I rode down the trail I chattered with God and admired His creation. I grimaced. *And I complained about Becky nearly all day.* Just like the rain leaking through my slicker, my ill thoughts toward Becky had slowly dripped into my life from the beginning of the summer. Each time she offended me, icy fingers of bitterness dug deeper into my heart until it froze into unforgiveness on the cold trail ride.

This attitude toward Becky had built a wall of ice between God and me. Just like the snow and ice had crusted over me, almost killing me, my resentments were causing spiritual hypothermia.

Slowly I wiggled my throbbing fingers. *Becky is not forcing me to feel this way. I'm choosing my responses.* I took a deep breath. "Lord, I choose to forgive her. Forgive me for my bitterness toward her." When I finished praying, warm peace settled in my heart.

After changing, I joined the hunters and crew in the cook tent. The guys dished up dinner for me. The warm food helped thaw my insides. After making sure I was going to be all right, the guys let me head for bed. Even though I snuggled deep into my sleeping bag, I couldn't sleep because of the intense burning on my hands and feet caused by frostbite.

For the next couple days I managed to do my duties even though my mind was in a fog and it took a long time for my body to realize it was okay and warm.

Forty-five days later I rode out of the wilderness. Back at the ranch, Becky and I sat down together. I was shocked to discover that many of the offenses I'd tallied were mistakes that fell through the cracks because of her busy schedule. I was more shocked when I learned that she thought I wanted her job. (No way! Who'd want to stay at the ranch instead of going out into the wilderness?) Although we didn't become best friends, we gained a new understanding that formed the foundation of a solid working relationship.

If you've had frostbite or come close to it, you know that even now my body is extremely sensitive to cold. In the summer my friends joke, "It must be 90 degrees. Rebecca finally quit wearing her wool sweater!" The redeeming point is that whenever I get cold, I'm reminded to make sure there's no ice between God and me.

> *Lord, I don't ever want to ice up with bitterness toward others, which ultimately separates me from You. Instead of counting offenses, give me the strength to turn away from them and reflect Your heart. Amen.*

22

Cowboy-Up

*Keep on loving each other as brothers and sisters.
Don't forget to show hospitality to strangers, for some who
have done this have entertained angels without realizing it!*

HEBREWS 13:1-2 NLT

The golden leaves of the cottonwood trees rattled in the light October breeze. Czar stood tied to the hitching rack at Monture Creek Camp, switching his tail to keep the flies away. Pushing his black mane aside, I brushed his neck with a soft-bristled brush. He closed his eyes and leaned into the brush, enjoying the massage. I whisked away clumps of dirt. "What should we do this morning?" I asked. I'd just finished making chocolate-chip cookies and chopping kindling, the last two items on my list of chores. The guides had taken the guests hunting, leaving camp empty. I looked around at the white canvas tents with their loosely tied door flaps gently blowing in the breeze. Without the guests sitting around the campfire and the guides bustling around doing chores, it looked like a ghost town. *Hollow. Hmmm. Hollow, that's how I feel on the inside.* A fly droned past and landed on Czar's hind leg. Stomping his foot, he switched his tail. The fly skittered away.

It was the third day of a 10-day outing. My pack season had started in May with trips to set up camp in Monture Creek. By June I was leading guests along rocky trails, and now I was the cook for hunting camp. Because I'd been in the mountains all summer and fall, I hadn't seen my friends. I missed hanging out with them. But most of all, I missed doing things *for* them. That was the hollowness that had settled in my soul. *But what can I do? I'm 14 miles into the wilderness— a world away from everybody.*

Czar's mane glistened in the sun. I pushed it back into place. "Jim and Karrie are going to be riding past today with their guests," I told Czar. "But they won't be stopping." I sighed. Jim and Karrie were outfitters and friends. We shared the same trailhead. My camp was 14 miles down the trail, and theirs was a grueling 24 miles. They didn't stop when they rode by because it took an extra hour to ride the quartermile off the main trail into my camp, tie the horses, sip coffee, round the guests back up, get mounted up, and hit the main trail. With 24 miles to ride, they didn't have an hour to spare.

I brushed Czar's black tail. "Any ideas?" I walked toward the threesided tack shed to get my saddle. A large piece of plywood caught my eye. A wild idea stampeded through my mind: *If they won't stop for cookies and coffee because it's too far out of the way, maybe I could bring some to them! That piece of plywood would make a great shelf in a tree.* Quickly I saddled Czar. We cantered out to the main trail where I eyed an enormous pine tree. Tipping my head from side to side, I sat figuring. *I need to put the shelf high enough that the deer won't eat the treats. What if I put it high enough that Jim and Karrie and their guests won't even have to dismount? What if they could ride up on their horses and serve themselves—like a drive-up window? Cowboy-Up Drive-Thru.* I giggled and rubbed Czar's neck. "Let's go get the tools and the plywood!"

When I returned to the trail with hardware supplies, I hammered the two-foot by three-foot plywood shelf in place. I stepped into the saddle and rode next to it. It was the perfect height to pour coffee on horseback. Delighted, I raced Czar back to camp for the fixings. When I got back, I stocked the shelf with Kool-Aid in a closed pitcher, chocolate-chip cookies in a plastic container, creamer, sugar, and an air-pot filled with coffee. I arranged napkins and paper cups so that each person could ride next to the shelf, dish up, and ride off. I weighted down the items so they wouldn't blow away. I pounded a nail into the tree above the shelf. Scribbling on a piece of notebook paper, I wrote, "Jim, Karrie, & Guests, Cowboy-up and help yourselves to treats. Love, Rebecca." Then I speared the note on the nail.

The leather squeaked as I climbed into the saddle. I laughed as I went through a trial-run at Cowboy-Up. I headed back to camp to start making dinner for my guests. I hummed as I browned hamburger in the skillet on the wood cookstove, imagining the shock on their faces when they discovered the wilderness drive-thru. The hollow feeling was gone, and my heart leaped with joy. The next morning, after drying the last of the breakfast dishes, I saddled Czar and cantered out to the trail. I beamed when I saw that the shelf was nearly empty. They'd eaten every cookie, drank all the Kool-Aid, and sipped every drop of coffee. They'd scribbled on the note, "Wow! What a surprise. Thank you!"

From that day on, I knew that no matter where I was—even in the middle of the wilderness, I could find opportunities to bless others. And that day was only the beginning of Cowboy-Up. Over the next few years, Jim, Karrie, and I had a blast with that shelf. It became a good-natured mystery. On the first day of each hunt, when Jim and Karrie rode out of the trailhead with their guests plodding behind them, they'd turn in their saddles and say, "In 14 miles we'll be briefly stop-ping at a drive-in and grabbing a snack." The guests, thinking they were getting their leg pulled, would roll their eyes and laugh. After miles of dusty trails through pine trees, across creeks, and around mountain-sides without seeing any signs of civilization, Jim and Karrie would remind them, "Keep your eyes open for that drive-in." The guests were convinced it was a joke. But when they rode their horses around the bend and saw the shelf with coffee and all the fixings, their eyes would bug out. Cowboy-Up always received rave reviews.

Lord, please show me opportunities to do things that will touch people's hearts. Amen.

23

Grizzly's Revenge

Dear friends, don't try to get even.
Let God take revenge.

ROMANS 12:19 CEV

The brisk November breeze tugged at the tree limbs. Larry rode his bay Arabian gelding across the mountain slope, leading a pack-saddled mule. I rode behind him. His saddle groaned as he turned and studied the terrain. He rode in a small circle, reined in, and then glanced back at me. Astonished he exclaimed, "It's gone! This is the spot where we left it." Stepping out of the saddle, he tied his horse to a tree. Carefully studying the ground, he walked in a semicircle.

I glanced at the pine-studded hillside. Snowberry brush grew in three-foot-high clumps. Dismounting, I tied Czar to a tree. One step at a time I eased my way across the slope, looking for clues. Today was the last day of a hunting trek. Last night before dusk, Larry's hunting guest shot a deer. They'd tagged and dressed it. Because it was too late to ride back to camp and get a mule to pack it out, they left the deer on the mountainside. This morning I'd asked Larry if I could ride with him when he went to pick it up. I loved exploring new country.

After helping the wranglers pack up camp, the guests and wranglers had turned their horses toward the trailhead. Larry and I mounted up, I grabbed the lead rope on a pack mule, and we headed up the mountain behind camp.

My boss bent over something in the dirt. "Wow! Look at this! I found the thief." I walked over and stared down. Larry pointed to the imprint of a huge oval pad with five toes above it. "It's a grizzly. Know how I can tell?"

I shook my head.

He pointed to an indentation several inches above the toes, "That is the end of one of his claws." He put his hand next to it. "His claws are as long as my fingers. A black bear has short claws."

The hair on the back of my head prickled. I'd heard stories of grizzlies sticking their claws into the crack above a car door and prying the door off its hinges. I looked around, hoping the critter wasn't close by.

Larry bent over, studying the ground. Step-by-step he worked out the trail. There were marks for 10 feet where the bear had dragged the deer. Then the bear, obviously massive, had probably slung the deer over his shoulder and walked off like it was carrying a knapsack. Larry rubbed his brown beard. "My hunter will want to know what happened. Let's go find that deer...or what's left of it."

We led our animals and bushwhacked on foot across the hillside. Studying the leaves on the bushes, we looked for drops of blood and checked every bent-over blade of grass. All I could think about was how that hunter had saved his money for years, bought an expensive license, paid for a guided hunt, and flown out here. He'd shot a nice deer, but this blasted bear had stolen it. The further we went, the angrier I got. After a half hour, the tracks led us to a fresh mound of dirt. Larry and I dug with our hands, tossing sticks and rocks to the side. We uncovered a half-eaten deer. The bear had buried it to keep the ravens and eagles from eating it so he could come back later to finish it off.

Larry rubbed his forehead. "I don't want to leave this deer because it'll give that grizzly a reason to hang around. This is too close to camp."

As we mantied the deer in canvas and loaded it onto the mule, I giggled. *It serves that bear right. He stole the deer in the first place. This'll make us even.* I watched Larry tighten the last sling rope, securing the load. A movement over his head caught my eye. Something circled in the sky. I squinted. Dozens of ravens lazily soared, and each circle seemed to move them closer to us. I pointed up. "What's that about?"

Larry looked. "Those birds are following the grizzly. They know it has buried a deer. When he unearths the deer, the ravens will swoop in for dinner." He glanced at the ravens coming our way. "It's time to get out of here."

We swung into our saddles and quickly picked our way across the hillside. The cawing of the ravens got louder and louder. I kept glancing over my shoulder, sweating as I watched those black birds. We bailed off the mountain, rode through camp, and boogied to the trailhead. Inside I still chuckled. We'd one-upped that bear.

At least that's what I thought—until I rode back into hunting camp three days later. The afternoon sun glistened off the pine needles as I rode alone. I was a couple hours ahead of the hunters so I could have dinner ready when they arrived. Czar picked up his pace as we turned off the main trail and onto the path that led to camp. He knew we were close to the end of the ride. I hummed as we wound through the pines and rode up to the hitching rack. Sliding to the ground, I scratched the little white star on Czar's forehead. "Ready for your grain?" I asked.

I walked over to the three-sided tack shed and gasped. The lid had been torn off the grain barrel. The barrel lay on its side—empty. Circling it, in the dirt, were grizzly tracks. *Oh no!* I ran toward the cook tent. The door flap of the tent was shredded. I ducked inside. The grizzly had explored with the power of a tornado. He'd pulled down my kitchen cupboard. Canned goods littered the floor. He'd swatted my kitchen boxes, sending them flying across the tent. Pots and pans lay strewn in the dirt. He'd knocked over the benches by the table. Even the 55-gallon-drum woodstove tilted at an awkward angle. That grizzly had returned to his deer...or where he'd left it, and then caught our scent. He'd tracked us to camp and left his message loud and clear: Don't mess with grizzlies.

Glancing at the crushed and scattered mess, I shook my head. I'd bragged that we'd scored points on him by claiming revenge. *But when has revenge ever worked? Never,* I thought. This time it had boomeranged. If we would've been in camp when that bear came in, he could have seriously injured or killed us.

Fortunately we never saw any signs of that bear for the rest of the year. The next day extremely cold weather moved in, and the grizzly bears went to bed for the winter. But I'll never forget what that bear taught me: Revenge is explosive.

Lord, when I'm tempted to speak or act out of hurt, remind
me that revenge is never the answer. Amen.

24

Midnight Ride

When I look at the night sky and see the work of your fingers—
the moon and the stars you have set in place—
what are people that you should think about them,
mere mortals that you should care for them? Yet you made them
only a little lower than God and crowned them with glory and honor.

PSALM 8:3-5 NLT

It was a dark and cool September night in the forest. So dark that I couldn't see my hands holding the reins. The sun had set, and neither the moon nor the stars had come out. The damp air groped through my wool jacket. The night was so still I could hear my breathing. Only the sound of my saddle horse's hooves plodding along the trail echoed through the pines. Tonight was the first time I'd be riding the 14 miles to camp through the mountains at night...and alone. I didn't know those miles would change me.

I was meeting up with the rest of the crew who had ridden in earlier today. Our goal was to put the finishing touches on setting up the hunting camp, cut and mark trails, and stack firewood so everything would be ready when we brought in guests next week. Because I had a stack of paperwork to finish, I'd sent the guys ahead and told them I'd be in by tomorrow. At eight o'clock I licked the last envelope and was too energized to go to bed. *I might as well ride into camp,* I decided. I drove to the corrals at the end of the road and tossed my saddle on Amarillo. I tied my slicker onto the saddle and tucked a flashlight into a saddlebag. With a tug, I tightened the cinch and then stepped into the stirrup just as the sun slipped behind the mountains. The whole world disappeared. The pitch-black forest engulfed me.

The sound of leather rubbing against leather made a comforting noise as I gently moved side to side in rhythm with Amarillo's gait. I reached down and stroked his neck. "I've never been anywhere this dark before. Are you sure you can see where we're going?" I wiggled my fingers. I couldn't see them. I brought my hand up to my face. Still nothing. I waved, blinked, and waved again. I couldn't detect any movement other than the little breeze from fanning the air. My heart raced. *Can Amarillo really see when it's this dark?*

I felt the muscles in Amarillo's body ripple as he climbed uphill. I awkwardly tilted my body forward a bit late because I couldn't see the terrain to anticipate what was coming next. His body turned left and then right as the trail wound through the trees. I felt like I was blind-folded and riding a slow-motion roller coaster. I had no idea where I was. *And neither does anyone else. What if I run into a problem?* My mind whirled. *That probably wasn't the smartest thing I've done...not telling anyone I was heading out.* Before, when I'd ridden this trail at night, I'd always had someone to talk with. Our chatter broke the emptiness and took the scariness out of the dark landscape. But tonight they gnawed at my heart. With each step deeper into the wilderness, my confidence eroded, leaving me uneasy and miserable.

Amarillo's body tipped downhill. He gathered his hindquarters underneath him to slow his pace. I leaned back. As he wove around a hill and into a gully, the gurgling song of a creek floated through the night air. *I know where we are! It's Yellowjacket Creek.* Amarillo's horseshoes clattered on pebbles. He splashed to the other side, and then we tipped uphill. I fretted. *It's going to be a long three hours to camp.* I already felt like I'd been in the saddle forever. Civilization seemed a lifetime away. The creek was only 45 minutes into the ride. The darkness had stripped everything from me: my vision, my sense of direction, and my balance. The further I rode, the more insignificant I felt.

Amarillo's body leveled out. I could feel the presence of a rock wall on my right side and a light breeze with the feeling of nothingness on my left. *Okay, we're riding along the cliff.* I straightened in the saddle and gripped my reins. "Take your time, boy," I encouraged. The sound of Amarillo's steps drifted across the valley 50 feet below. A small stone dislodged by his foot fell off the trail and plunged down the cliff. Ping...ping...ping. The bottom was so far down that it seemed to take forever before the sound stopped. I braced myself, holding my balance in the center of the saddle. Finally on both sides of me I heard the breeze lightly whispering through the pines. *Okay, we're back on the flats.* I breathed a sigh of relief.

I tipped my head back and stared into the sky. The first star twinkled from millions of miles away. Then a few more appeared. Soon the Milky Way studded the sky. I frowned. *I am such a small part of this galaxy.* The moon glowed from behind a mountain to the east. The sky transformed from black to a deep cobalt blue. As the full moon rose, the trees seemed to grow taller, towering over me, their tops outlined against the sky. I felt small, like a speck of dust. I looked at the moon. *If anyone is standing on the moon, I sure wouldn't know it. They'd be just a tiny dot, invisible to my eyes.* And then I thought of God sitting in heaven and looking at the earth. *Lord, who am I? I'm merely one person riding her horse down a trail in the middle of the night—somewhere on this enormous planet in the Milky Way Galaxy.*

God's resounding voice echoed through my spirit: "You're significant to Me. I created you."

I felt like saying "I know," but did I really? I could quote all the right scriptures and say the correct words. But if I believed, why did I question it sometimes? It was because the words were just in my head; my heart hadn't settled the matter. *Lord, help me believe.*

God's voice came to me again: "I created all this for you. Sit back and enjoy it."

My saddle squeaked as I wiggled around getting comfortable. I leaned back, relaxed. A coyote howled. Its eerie call drifted over the mountain. A cool breeze rustled through the pines, making the evening smell like Christmas. From across the valley another coyote answered the first. God had taken me by the hand and led me into His theater. The curtain had been raised. It was as if He was excitedly showing me "Night" for the first time.

The angle of the brilliant moon created a tall shadow of Amarillo and me on the trail. Instead of feeling dwarfed and small, I laughed and held my arms at angles, creating funny-shaped shadows. My loneliness and fear had vanished.

Amarillo moved into a small clearing. The silvery moonlight illuminated several deer munching on grass. One lifted its head and watched us ride by before nonchalantly returning to eating. The trail led into a long, straight corridor through the forest. An owl hooted, "Whooo... whooo." I heard a whooshing sound overhead and glanced up. The hunting bird swooped down 100 feet in front of me and snatched dinner. It flew to a nearby treetop. In the moonlight I watched it eat as I rode past. The next few hours passed quickly as I delightedly watched and listened as creation unfolded all around me.

When Amarillo turned into the hunting camp, I tipped my head back and looked into the sky. Thousands of stars were twinkling now. I'd once heard from a friend that stars are the twinkles in God's eyes. I grinned. I knew He'd been delighted to share "Night" with me, and I'd thoroughly enjoyed it.

Lord, when I feel insignificant, please remind me that You delight in watching me enjoy this world You created. Amen.

25

Pack-String Express

*They heard the sound of the LORD God walking in the garden
in the cool of the day...Then the LORD God called to Adam
and said to him, "Where are you?"*

GENESIS 3:8-9

I cantered Czar through the tan grass of Danaher Valley. The crisp
October air carried the scent of mountain pines mingled with the
sweet smell of aspens. I gazed at the brilliant-red huckleberry bushes
covering the hillsides. *Fall is my favorite season,* I thought. I shifted
my weight in the saddle as I reined Czar up the trail toward hunting camp. His feet trod easily up the well-used trail. In just a couple
hours the crew would lead in the next group of guests, along with the
pack mule strings loaded with supplies for another hunt. And best of
all would be mail.

I slowed Czar to a walk as we crested the hill. A cluster of tents
dotted the grassy bench. At the thought of mail, my heart leaped. I
hadn't been in "civilization" for more than 40 days, and the last four
days I'd been in camp alone. In the beginning of September I'd ridden
the 24 miles into Danaher Camp, and I wouldn't ride out until the end

of November. The only contact I had with family, friends, and the world was by mail and the scraps of news the crew and guests shared.

I tied Czar to the hitching rack, unsaddled him, and gave him grain. The whole time I speculated about who had written to me. I grinned as I imagined Darrin, one of the wranglers, handing me a fat packet of letters. Karen, my boss, always tucked them in a plastic bread bag to keep them clean and dry. I loved the notes from my mom telling me about her blooming garden and the waves that crashed against the shore at their lake home. Jean shared about the guests at the ranch where she worked. And Jeanne usually wrote about her kids' adventures. Nothing earth-shattering—just chitchat—but I read every note over and over again until the edges were tattered and the folded creases gave way to holes.

Turning Czar loose in the pole corral, I hurried to the cook tent to put the pot roast on the stove and the bread in the oven. It seemed like only moments passed before Czar whinnied a hello that was soon followed by the chatter of guests and the hoofbeats of horses and mules. I slipped into my green fleece jacket and hustled to the corral.

Guests stiffly dismounted after their long ride. I warmly welcomed them, and then the trail boss led them to their tents. I walked over to the wranglers who were untying the loads from the mules. "Hey, guys, how was the trip?"

Darrin lifted a load off a mule. "Uneventful. How was your time alone?"

"Great, but I'm really looking forward to reading my mail after we finish unsaddling."

Darrin handed me the lead rope of a mule ready to be taken to the corral. "I bet you are."

The next hour I helped slip the loads off mules, unsaddle, and turn them loose in the corral. After I let go of the last mule, Darrin dug in his saddlebags and pulled out the bread bag. I opened it. Only a note from Karen, food lists for the next trip, and a list of names and other information about the guests were in there. "Any other mail?" I asked hopefully.

"Nope. That's it."

Tears stung my eyes. I bit my lip. *Nobody wrote—not even Mom?* I wanted to run to my tent and slink into the bottom of my sleeping bag. But I had to cook dinner for 12, haul 50 gallons of water from the creek, and wash the dishes. Then I'd have to unpack and put away the six mule-loads of canned goods, produce, and camp supplies. I'd be lucky to finish my cook chores and retreat to my tent before midnight.

Stumbling to the cook tent, I stoked the woodstove and finished slapping dinner together. I unfolded Karen's note. "Remember to inventory leftover produce after this hunt. I'd write more, but I'm out of time. Karen." Just a business note. No chitchat. Disappointment filled my soul.

I called the guests to dinner and faked a smile as they wandered through the buffet line, heaping mashed potatoes, gravy, and meat onto their plates. Dinner conversation was filled with mindless chatter as I drifted in my own world of hurt. *Why didn't anyone write?*

The crew and guests filtered to their tents to unpack, leaving me alone. Stacks of dirty dishes cluttered the cupboards and the new boxes of groceries littered the floor. I sighed as I poured a kettle of steaming water into the sink and washed dishes. *No mail. Why? I've been writing everyone. All I wanted was a "hello." Is that too much to ask? God, why didn't anyone write?*

Then it struck me. *When was the last time I chitchatted with God?* I paused and then talked to Him. *When was the last time I talked to You without whining or begging for something?* My mind drifted to one of my favorite Bible verses in Genesis. God is looking for Adam in the garden. He was disappointed when Adam didn't rush out to walk with Him. *What were those walks with God like? Perhaps Adam told God how much he loved riding a horse through the garden in the cool of the day. Just chitchatting and enjoying walking side-by-side with God. Father in heaven, I'm so sorry. I don't want to be a fair-weather friend. I want to always have You by my side.*

While drying dishes and unpacking supplies I chattered in my mind. *God, I love being in hunting camp. The aspens are so beautiful with their vibrant gold leaves. I love the way You painted the clouds crimson during the sunset tonight.* Hours later I lifted the cardboard lid off the last box of groceries. Lying neatly on top was a bread bag bursting with mail! The first letter was from Mom. And then I saw one from Karen, and Jean, and Jeanne, and many more. Tears streamed down my face. I poured a cup of coffee, sat at the plank table, and read each letter twice.

Thank You, Lord, for reminding me that You want to share my days—even in chitchat about what's going on in my life. Amen.

26

Laughter

*He will yet fill your mouth with laughter and
your lips with shouts of joy.*

JOB 8:21

The obnoxious rumbling snore woke me. *Not again!* "Roll over, Jeff," I growled under my breath as I grabbed the top of my sleeping bag and pulled it over my head. I rolled to the far edge of my hay-stuffed bed that was situated on top of hay bales. The snoring crescendoed, punctuated by a few snorts. *AArrrggghhh!* This was ridiculous. Jeff had just started working for our outfit. His nocturnal habits were more annoying than dealing with the guests, bears, deer, horses, and mules combined. He slept in the crew tent about 50 feet across camp from my place, but his snoring sounded like a megaphone blasting in my ear.

I pounded my fist into the hay. *God, I need rest. Help me.* It had been a grueling summer leading guests through the wilderness on pack trips. On summer trips I never really fell into deep sleep because I was always alert for bears, runaway horses, guests that might need something, and the deer that loved to sneak into camp and break into the bread boxes. My body longed to stay prone for hours on end. I'd thought I could do that on this crew-only trip. The days would be easy as we went about setting up the camp and cutting out trails. The horses were in the corral for the night, and the bears probably didn't know we'd packed in groceries yet. All I wanted were multiple zzzzz's, but Jeff's snoring was destroying my hopes. I wanted to storm over to the crew tent and stuff hay into his mouth.

The next morning the flaps of the white canvas cook tent rustled in the breeze. The wranglers and I rubbed our eyes and sipped coffee as we sat around the kitchen table covered with a red-checkered tablecloth. I don't think any of us got a lick of sleep. I was beginning to wonder if there should be a question on the job application like "On a scale of 1 to 10, how loud is your snoring?"

The coffeepot simmered on the stove. The heat and silence were lulling us to sleep. I reached down and picked up my yellow tiger cat named Hamster. The abundance of food in hunting camp lured mice from miles around, so we'd packed in Hamster to serve as our mobile mouse control.

When Jeff strolled in, the wranglers groaned. I announced, "You snored so loudly your tent flapped. I thought it was going to fly away." The guys chuckled. Jeff shrugged his shoulders and stroked his long, dark beard. "How would you know?" he asked.

I petted Hamster as I sourly said, "Because you kept me awake— again." The guys murmured and nodded their heads. After breakfast we saddled the horses, loaded the chainsaws on the mules, and rode up the mountain behind camp to cut hunting trails. By the time the last rays of the sun settled on the horizon, I flopped into bed exhausted. Hamster curled up next to me. It seemed like I'd barely gotten to sleep when a roar blasted through camp. I woke up, realized it was Jeff's snoring, and yanked my sleeping bag over my head.

Then I heard one of the guys whisper loudly, "Jeff! Hey, Jeff."

The snoring continued.

"Jeff! Jeff, roll over!"

The rhythmic snoring got louder.

Then I heard a thud. A couple of snorts followed...and then golden silence.

I wondered if someone had thrown something at the guy. That's what it sounded like. I breathed a sigh of relief and poked my head out of my sleeping bag. But just as I was drifting into zzzzz land, the snoring resounded through the clear night. Once again I heard a thud, a couple of snorts, and then beautiful silence...but not for long. *This better not keep up all fall. None of us will get any sleep. God, help! I crave and need sleep.*

The snoring echoed through the wilderness.

Suddenly Jeff screamed.

I sat straight up in bed. My hair prickled.

Suddenly I heard the guys laughing.

I chuckled and rolled over to catch some sleep. I knew they'd tell me the story over breakfast.

The next morning in the cook tent, I flipped pancakes on the cast-iron griddle. As the crew walked through the tent flap, they laughed and slapped each other on the back. Bob, one of the wranglers, was laughing so hard he could barely stand. "Rebecca, you would have loved to have been there. Hamster snuck into our tent. He poked around a bit and then jumped up on Jeff's cot. Jeff's beard must have looked warm because Hamster snuggled under it." Bob and the guys grabbed their guts and howled with laughter. "When Jeff started snoring, Hamster bolted awake, stood on Jeff's chest, and peered into his mouth. Hamster must have been confused by the noise because he cocked his head side to side as the snores rolled out, making Jeff's tonsils rattle. The cat must have decided that those tonsils were some kind of a mouse. He pounced—sticking both front paws into Jeff's mouth!" All of us rocked with laughter. Bob wiped the tears from his eyes and continued. "Then Jeff clawed Hamster out of his mouth and screamed."

Even Jeff laughed and chimed in, "Yeah, then you guys fell sound asleep, but I was awake all night."

The rest of the fall, Hamster stayed on snore patrol and taught Jeff to sleep on his side. In a strange way Hamster was an answer to prayer. I wonder if God laughed Himself silly when He brainstormed the idea. God showed me, through Hamster, that by using humor to deal with conflict, no one would be offended. Instead our shared laughter bonded us together into a solid, caring team.

Thank You, Lord, for giving us laughter to solve our conflicts, lighten our burdens, and knit us together as friends. Amen.

27

Keeping Time

*Whatever you do, work at it with all your heart,
as working for the Lord, not for men.*

COLOSSIANS 3:23

A light breeze blew as I surveyed the mountainside. I was working as a ranger, riding the wilderness to assess its health and check on campers and camps. I reined Czar to a stop at a fork in the trail. Little Girl, my brown pack mule who was walking behind us, lowered her head. Using her agile lips like fingers, she grasped a long stalk of grass and looped it into her mouth with her tongue. I looked at the fork and wondered, *Do I have time to ride up to Sarbo or should I stay in the valley bottom? The valley bottom will only take two hours to inventory. But if I go up Sarbo, it's a four-hour, round-trip ride and maybe an hour to check things out.* I pushed back my black cowboy hat and squinted at the sun. *What time is it?* I couldn't tell because it was the end of June, the time of summer solstice. Daybreak was at four thirty and sunset at ten. *I wish I hadn't lost my watch,* I thought.

When I had camped by Cabin Creek, I'd taken off my watch and set it next to me while I knelt by water and washed up before bed. I didn't remember it until the next morning, and I then couldn't find it. I didn't miss the watch very much the first few days, but I sure did today. It was the sixth day of a ten-day trek into the woods for the U.S. Forest Service (USFS). Czar, Little Girl, my black German Shepherd, Rye, and I were alone. I liked the hours best. When I outfitted, work had started before sunup and ended after sunset, the average workday about 18 hours long. But the USFS required only an eight-hour day.

Czar's neck glistened with sweat. I stroked it and looked at the position of the sun. One o'clock? Or is it later? If it's one o'clock, and I do the valley, I'll finish my day too early. If it's later and I ride up to Sarbo, I'll finish a little late. Glancing up the draw toward Sarbo, I reasoned, "But Sarbo is out of the way. There shouldn't be too much trash to clean up." Little Girl rubbed her head on Czar's rear. Czar stomped his foot and shook his head at her. I flicked the lead rope toward Little Girl and she backed up. I patted Czar's neck to calm him down. "Let's go," I announced, guiding him up one side of the trail.

The next two hours hooves and paws clopped and padded up the trail that wound through a mosaic burn. Stands of green pines stood in clusters next to scorched earth studded with charred pines. It was almost as if someone had drawn a line through the forest; one side toasted and the other stayed green. The trail skirted the steep hillside covered with huckleberry and snowberry bushes and then crossed a stretch of burn. I looked at the blackened earth. A thin, gray-looking ribbon lay next to the trail. I groaned. *Argh. Telegraph wire.* Before the advent of radios, the USFS had strung telegraph wire from their cabins in the wilderness to the ranger stations. *And part of my job was ridding the forest of debris, so I would have to pack it out. What a pain.* In my mind I could see grains of sand slipping through an hourglass. *I'll get it on the way back,* I decided.

The trail turned and followed the draw into Sarbo. When we rode into the high mountain basin rimmed by rock walls, pikas whistled a warning and scurried for their burrows. A small herd of deer grazing next to a rock wall lifted their heads and twitched their tails. Czar walked into a stand of trees as I glanced at the sun. Although it was still high in the sky, it now tipped toward the mountains. *I bet it's after four.* I tied Czar and Little Girl to trees and dug a map out of my saddlebags. It crinkled as I unfolded it to find the "X" that marked the campsite I was to check.

Taking bearings from the rim of the mountain and the sun, I hiked to the other side of the basin and into the burn. I poked around the charred remains next to several blackened pines. An odd-looking, black-textured something poked an inch above the ash between the trees. I kicked it with my boot. Clunk. It sounded like a piece of heavy metal. With the toe of my boot, I carved away the ash and tugged. Out came a cast-iron-woodstove door weighing at least 20 pounds. I heaved the door aside. Scooping away more ash, I unearthed a small cast iron stove. I grunted as I rolled it out of the hole. *This thing must weigh 60 pounds.* I eyed the hole and groaned. It was filled with broken glass bottles and rusty cans.

What next? I fussed as I looked at the sun slipping into the western sky. *Why did I come up here today? If only I'd had my watch!* I pulled a rusty can out of the ground. *This is going to take hours. I might not get back to camp before dark. Maybe I should ride out now and come back in the morning.* I sighed. That would waste four hours travel time. I walked over to Little Girl and pulled the shovel off her saddle.

The next couple hours I dug out cans and bottles. I mantied them into loads that looked like overstuffed Santa sacks. The cans clattered when I slung them on Little Girl's saddle. Hefting the stove on top, I sandwiched it between the two packs and lashed it down. Whistling for Rye, I glanced at the sun. *It must be close to seven, and I still have to pick up the wire.* In my mind a time clock flashed "Overtime!"

Rye tagged at my heels as I led Little Girl over to Czar and swung into the saddle. The sunlight filtered sideways through the trees as we rumbled down the dusty trail, the cans rattling with each step. When we came to the downed telegraph wire I dug my wire cutters out of the saddlebags and followed the gray ribbon of wire through the ash and up a short hill. I tried to wrestle the stiff wire into a roll, but instead of coiling, it sprang into a rat's nest. I tied four of those tangled balls onto Little Girl's loads, patted her, and frowned. "You look like an old peddler's mule with the axe, saw, and shovel poking out and that cast iron stove stuffed on top, along with the tangled mess of wire."

I swung into the saddle and turned to watch the loads rock as Little Girl walked. They looked even. I eyed the sun again. *I bet it's close to eight thirty.* I pushed Czar into a faster walk. Within a couple steps, the packs on Little Girl rattled and banged. They wobbled and threatened to slip off-center. I slowed Czar to a crawl and growled, "The USFS is getting their money's worth today."

The trail wound through brushy draws and small meadows. Nervously I watched the packs. Czar and Little Girl's hooves clattered on the rocky trail as it narrowed to four-feet wide, funneling next to a steep wall. The right side dropped down a cliff into a canyon. Fifty yards later I glanced at the packs and grimaced. The D ring of the packsaddle had tipped off center. I eyed the steep slope. *If the saddle rolls under Little Girl's belly, it'll pull her off balance and off the cliff.* I studied the trail. It wasn't wide enough for me to reload her. I glanced in front of me. *Will the packs ride okay until we get to the flat?* With each step the stove shifted, pushing the saddle toward the drop-off side.

What am I going to do? I don't have room to adjust the packs, but I can't let them roll and watch her tumble off the cliff. I glanced at the sun slipping behind the mountain. *Blast! I've got to do something now. If I can get that saddle to move a couple inches toward center at least they won't roll while she's on the cliff.* A crazy idea sparked in my mind. I reined Czar to a stop and stepped off the left side of the saddle and onto the rocky slope above him. I teetered while I bent over and wrapped his reins around the saddle, to keep him from stepping on them. I warned him, "Don't you dare leave the country."

Little Girl eyed me as I shinnied across the slope above her. Firmly grabbing a bush to steady myself, I dug my left foot into the slope. Stones dislodged and clattered down. With my right foot, I gently stepped onto Little Girl's pack. Hunched over, I straddled between the slope and her pack, holding my breath and waiting to see what she'd do. Little Girl's long, fuzzy, brown ears swiveled like periscopes, but she didn't move. I breathed a sigh of relief. "Good girl," I encouraged. Slowly I drew my left foot off the bank, lifted it over the nest of wire, and put it on her pack. I moved my other foot onto the other pack.

Little Girl turned her head and batted her long, black eyelashes as if saying, "Are you feeling okay?" Glancing at a mouthwatering tuft of grass, she took a step forward to snatch it. Her motion caused me to wobble. Standing on top of her packs, I threw my arms out to my sides for balance. Glancing down the cliff, the blood drained out of my face. I gritted my teeth and said, "Will you please stand still!"

She stopped and munched. I slid both of my feet onto the left pack, put both my arms out for balance, held my breath, and then jumped. The D ring inched to the left. Little Girl didn't do anything except munch long stems of grass. I grinned. Once again I pounded my weight onto the left pack. The D ring slipped to the center just as Little Girl spied another bunch of grass, and moseyed toward it. I lurched backward, almost losing my balance. I screeched, "Will you do your job and stand still!"

I suddenly realized something. *What more could I ask of Little Girl? What other mule would allow me to load packs that rattled, tie on goofy-looking balls of wire, and add a heavy woodstove? And then let me climb on top—while standing on a cliff, and jump up and down—without freaking out? She was doing her job. She'd been giving me her whole heart since this morning. In fact, she'd been doing that more than I was.*

My struggle really hadn't been about losing my watch. Instead it was a heart issue. I'd been watching the sun, trying to dole out just the right amount of work to satisfy the USFS without giving them any extra. Instead, I should have thrown my heart into my work so when I crawled into my hammock in the evening, I would feel satisfied with what I'd accomplished.

Little Girl nibbled a couple blades of grass. I jumped off her packs and onto the steep slope. I clawed my way in front of her and slid to the ground. Rubbing her forehead I said, "You're quite a mule! Now, let's get off this cliff."

For the rest of my hitch at the Forest Service I set goals that stretched me. One night I pitched my tent in the same spot where I'd lost my watch. While kneeling next to the stream washing up before bed, my eye caught a glimmer in the grass. My watch! I picked it up and stared at it. The second hand was still going around. I grinned and thought, *I lost my watch—until I found my integrity.*

The rest of the summer and fall I tucked my watch into the saddlebags. At the end of the season, I was shocked and pleasantly surprised when the USFS awarded me a Certificate of Merit for the wilderness work I'd accomplished.

Lord, thank You for teaching me that it's not about the hours I put into a project; it's about how much of my heart I'm giving. Amen.

28

Frozen Long Johns

Yet they did not listen or pay attention;
they were stiff-necked and would not listen.

JEREMIAH 17:23

Only a few stars twinkled in the black sky. My boots crunched through the snow as I trudged to my white canvas wall tent, the wire handle of a Coleman gas lantern looped over my arm. The lantern hissed and cast a golden glow across the landscape in Cooney Creek Camp. I growled as I pushed the tent flap aside and stooped low to duck inside. "This thing is the size of an overgrown outhouse!" I muttered. I hung the lantern just inside the door on the hook that was in the ridge pole. The door on the itty-bitty woodstove creaked as I opened it and laid kindling. I was only able to squeeze one small split log on top. Peeling off my gloves, I poured diesel fuel on the kindling and lit a match. The flames licked the wood, and I closed the stove door. *Why am I even lighting a fire?* The tent was so small only a miniature stove would fit in it, and the stove was so small it could only hold enough wood to burn for an hour.

I plunked down on my cot. Even though it was against the wall,

126

my knees were only two feet from the stove. Because I was the camp cook, boxes of canned goods were stacked floor to ceiling along the opposite wall, leaving a skinny aisle between the boxes and my cot. Last year's tent had been large enough for me to build shelves to stack my clothes and put out some personal items, but this tent only had room for me to squeeze my duffel in the corner. *Why is everything I want out of that duffel bag always at the bottom?* I groused. *I'm sick of digging through it.*

The fire crackled and popped. Heat rolled off the stove. Stretching out my hands, I warmed them until I heard the log settle. Standing up to add another small log, I whacked my head on the lantern. "Ouch!" I rubbed my head. *I can't wait to let the boss have it with both barrels when he rides in tomorrow. He knew I was going to live in this tent from September until the end of November. What was wrong with last year's tent?* Boiling, I mulled over confronting Jack tomorrow. He'd been guiding out of a different hunting camp for the last month and a half so I hadn't seen him since I got here.

I slammed a log into the stove and closed down the damper. In an hour, when the fire went out, the temperature in the tent would plummet to match the outside temperature. Tonight it would get down to 10 degrees. Worse yet, I'd gotten frostbite on my face, fingers, and toes so many times that I couldn't keep them warm enough to not hurt. Often I'd get so cold my bones would ache. *I'd better bundle up.* I stood over my duffel and dug clothes out like a dog digging under a fence: long john pants, two pairs of wool socks, sweat pants, long john top, turtleneck, wool scarf, wool sweater, and a wool stocking cap. *This is ridiculous. Jack could have chosen a decent-sized tent for me.* I felt like I was being punished.

After bundling up into the size of an abominable snowman, I crawled into my red mummy sleeping bag that was stuffed into another sleeping bag and covered with a canvas tarp. I drew the second sleeping bag and canvas over my head to keep my nose from being frostbitten. For extra measure, I pulled the drawstring of my mummy bag tight.

The bag wrapped around my head like a hood, leaving a tiny hole for my nose and mouth. In minutes I drifted off to sleep.

At four o'clock the alarm clock blared. I quickly reached my arm out of the warm sleeping bag, slapped the snooze bar, and burrowed into the bottom of the heap. A cold draft blasted into my sleeping bag. "Brrr." I cringed as I thought about jumping out of bed to cook breakfast for the six ravenous hunters and three guides. *If I were in one of those spacious crew tents, my stove would still be burning and it'd be warm.* The alarm clock beeped again. I smacked it off. *Now or never.* I flicked on my flashlight, slipped my feet into my winter boots, and leaped for my jacket that was hanging on a nail by the doorpost. When I stood up I smacked my head on the Coleman lantern again. *Dumb tent...dumb boss!* I lifted the lantern off the hook. The metal was so cold it burned my hands when I pumped it up to pressure. My icy fingers fumbled with a match and the lantern hissed to life. Gratefully I buried my hands in wool mittens and wrestled my way through the itty-bitty tent door.

Smoke from the woodstoves in the guest tents hung in the air as I crunched through the snow to the cook tent. *Must be nice to sleep in a warm place.* Everything in the cook tent was frigid. I laid the kindling in the stove as quickly as I could and struck the match. While frying bacon I held my hands over the heat to warm them, but they didn't thaw out until the large pot of coffee came to a boil.

By the time I tossed together breakfast, sent the hunters out the door with sack lunches, and washed dishes, the sun was poking over the mountain and turning the valley into a winter wonderland. Frost coated every needle on the pine trees. Each twig of the willows dripped with crystals. There wasn't a cloud in the blue sky, and the sun radiated off the snow. *A perfect day for a horseback ride. But there's one thing I have to do first.*

I trudged to my tent. Squeezing through the door, I pulled my spare long johns out of the dirty clothes bag. It was going to warm up this afternoon, maybe even get in the 40s. It would be my last chance to wash and hang the long johns outside to dry. *If I had last year's tent I could have hung them inside to dry. But not this tent. There's no room. They'd drip all over my sleeping bags.* I swished them in a wash pan, wrung them out, and hung them to dry on a clothesline strung between two trees behind my tent so they'd be out of sight. Then I raced down to the corral.

Czar hung his head over the fence and nickered to me. I rubbed the star on his forehead. "Are you ready for a ride?" I slid between the wooden rails and bridled him. After cinching on the saddle, I swung up and we headed down the trail. The sun's rays glittered from the snowflakes. The fresh scent of clean air laden with snow rolled off the peaks. Frost fell from twigs and lazily drifted onto the trail. As peaceful as it looked, I didn't enjoy it. Instead I was rehearsing the venomous words I would spew at my boss. *Maybe I could sneak in a sarcastic comment like "Are the miniature tents only for cooks?"* I leaned forward and rubbed Czar's neck. "What do you think? He's made my life miserable all fall with that itty-bitty cell of a tent. Tonight I'll see him for the first time..." I raised my eyebrows and lowered my voice, "...since the dastardly deed." I mulled over what to say until we rode back into camp.

All afternoon while chopping kindling and refueling the gas lanterns, I honed my speech. The opportunity arose after dinner. The guests had stuffed themselves and filtered back to their nice warm tents. I stood in the cook tent stacking dirty dishes. The guides and Jack sat at the plank table drinking coffee and studying hunting maps while discussing tomorrow's game plan. When they finished, Jack picked up their coffee cups and set them on the counter. He ran his fingers through his white hair and asked, "Rebecca, how have you been doing? The hunters have been raving about your cooking."

I looked at my boots. "I've really enjoyed the hunters. But the first few hunts I got incredibly exhausted. I had to wake up every couple hours to stoke that silly little stove." I took a deep breath and blurted, "That tent's way too small. I feel like a caged rat. What was wrong with last year's tent?"

Jack frowned. "The day we were packing the gear, I pulled it off the shelf and discovered that over the winter it had rotted." Jack smoothed his moustache. "This tent was the only other one we had."

My face flushed. Quickly I gathered a stack of plates and set them in the sink. They rattled and glugged into the soapy dishwater. After cleaning up the kitchen in record time, I shrugged into my winter jacket. I walked through the cook tent, turning off all but one of the lanterns. The lantern I held hissed as I stepped out of the tent into the black night. The air was so cold it sucked the breath out of me. *And my tent is this cold.*

Snow squeaked with each footstep. From the way it sounded, the temperature had dipped below zero already. Untying my tent door flap, I remembered my long johns. I walked behind the tent. The glow of the lantern illuminated a sheet of ice on the clothesline. My jaw dropped. They were frozen—spread eagle. I tried pinching the clothespins open, but they were frozen solid. *If I had a decent tent I wouldn't be out here freezing, trying to get this off that line,* I murmured. I tried using both hands to pinch the clothespins open, but it was like they were super-glued. Setting the lantern in the snow, I grabbed the long johns by the ankles and jerked. Whop! They came loose from the clothesline and fell like a chunk of lead into the snow.

Steam rose from my breath as I picked up the lantern with my left hand. Reaching down with my right, I picked up the board-like long johns. Carrying them by the top, I walked to the front of the tent and pushed that itty-bitty tent flap open a crack. Waves of heat rolled off the lantern. Holding it so that it wouldn't burn a hole in the tent, I held the long johns in my right hand and tried to manipulate them through the door...but the outstretched legs were wider than the tent flap. I tried using my knee to poke the legs through that small hole. I got one leg in. Then the other leg caught on the tent frame. *This is ridiculous!*

I backed out of the tent and turned the long johns sideways, carrying them like a suitcase. This time one leg hung up on my duffel bag and I tripped. *I hope nobody's watching me dance with frozen underwear!* Suddenly I broke out laughing. *I'm dancing with long johns because they're stiff. They're not flexible at all. Not flexible...* Something reverberated in my mind. Hmmm...the long johns were exactly like my frozen attitude about this tent. *My* attitude was making my life miserable, not Jack choosing this tent. He wasn't punishing me. It was the only tent available. Instead of immediately taking offense, I could have chosen to believe the best about the situation. I could have been grateful that I had my own tent, rather than the other option of sleeping in the cook tent and not having any privacy.

After slowly and finally squeezing the long johns through the door, I giggled. *I bet I'm the only girl who danced with a pair of long johns tonight.* Stuffing small chunks of wood into my itty-bitty woodstove, I made a plan. *On extremely cold nights I'm going to set the alarm every hour. I might be exhausted in the morning, but it's going to work out just fine.*

> *Lord, when I'm in a challenging situation, please remind me to look for the solution rather than wallowing in perceived offenses. Amen.*

29

Grizzly in Camp

Do not be afraid of the terrors of the night.

PSALM 91:5 NLT

In the white canvas cook tent, waves of heat emanated from the wood-stove. Traditionally the last night in hunting camp gets pretty loud, and this night was no exception. Eleven of us, crew and guests, ate steak dinners around the long plank table. We hooted and hollered, trying to "one up" each other as we swapped stories of our adventures during the past nine days. Suddenly the tent flap parted. A frigid breeze blasted through as a wool-gloved hand holding a Coleman gas lantern appeared. Darrin stepped trancelike into the tent. Snowflakes clung to the wrangler's winter jacket. The light of the lantern eerily illuminated his face. "I was on the way to the corrals to feed the horses, and I almost tripped over a grizzly."

Everyone stopped mid-motion. We stared at each other. Only the hiss of the lanterns broke the silence. Jack ran his hand through his white hair. "Let's check it out." Jack and the guides shrugged on their jackets and pulled on their hats. They grabbed guns and lanterns and then stormed the corrals to check on the horses…and to track the beast.

The plastic plates rattled in the sink as I scrubbed them, my imagination running wild. Cooney Creek Camp, 17 long horseback miles into the wilderness, consisted of a half dozen white canvas wall tents pitched in a grassy meadow rimmed by cliffs that funneled all trails through the center of camp, including the grizzly migration trail. Tomorrow everyone would ride for home except me. I was staying four more days and three nights. My job? To keep the grizzlies out of camp...and they were migrating right now.

A half-hour later Jack and the guides stomped snow off their boots as they stepped into the cook tent. I asked, "What's up?"

Darrin replied, "The horses are bunched in the corral corner snorting. But they're fine."

Jack poured himself a cup of coffee. "What kind of bear is this? He wasn't cautious at all." Jack paced. "That bear boldly checked out the entire camp...and the lanterns were lit in all the tents *and* at the corrals. All of us were hooting and hollering too." He stroked his moustache and nodded his head. "He'll be back, I'm sure. He found dinner—he dredged the dishwater pit."

I retreated to my tent and lay on my cot with my eyes wide open. The biological name for the grizzly, *Ursus arctos horribilis,* translates into "horrible northern bear." It has a reputation of being one of the most ferocious and dangerous mammals in North America. I shuddered as I thought about their attributes. They are nocturnal. *I can't see that well at night.* They can outrun a horse in a quarter mile. *Not me; I'm the poky puppy.* The notorious hump on their back is a mass of muscle that enables them to use their paws with stunning striking force. I'd seen videos of grizzlies running through a herd of elk, swatting their heads and killing them with single blows. Because of their thick layer of fat and slow metabolism, it's hard to shoot them *dead* before they get to you. And I knew they could use their four-inch-long front claws like a can opener when prying open an automobile. *All I have is a thin sheet of canvas between the bears and me.*

After breakfast I walked to the corrals to say goodbye to the guests and crew. Jack tossed his saddle on his mule. While tightening the cinch he asked, under his breath, "Have you got enough ammo?"

I nodded. My heart pounded as he swung his leg over the saddle. He glanced at me compassionately and said, "Watch out for that bear."

The guests mounted their horses. Jack reined his mule down the trail and shouted to the guests, "We're burning daylight."

The guests tipped their hats as they rode past me, followed by wranglers leading the strings of mules. I watched until the last mule disappeared around a bend. I kicked my toe in the dirt. *It's going to be a long four days.*

I busied myself chopping kindling. With each swing of the axe I reviewed the facts. Grizzlies gorge themselves in the fall to put on a thick layer of fat that feeds their body all winter while they hibernate. It had been a dry year so berries and their normal food sources were scarce. This bear had eaten a buffet in our camp last night. *He'd be stupid not to come back.* I was sleeping in the grocery tent this trip. My nightstand was a wooden kitchen box brimming with candy bars.

All day long that grizzly terrorized my mind. While pouring Coleman fuel into the lanterns, I summed up my resources: one 12-gauge shotgun, one .357 pistol, two cans of bear spray, and my German shepherd, Rye. Dogs aren't much use against a grizzly. I'd have to keep her tied to my tent, but at least she'd growl and wake me when the bear came by. I hoped so anyway.

The afternoon lagged. I bundled up my sleeping bag and carried it into a guest tent, far away from the groceries. By dinner I was emotionally exhausted. I plunked down at the kitchen table and sipped chicken soup. I browsed through the stack of mail that had come with the pack string. Thumbing through a magazine from one of my favorite ministries, an article caught my eye. It was about the protection found in Psalm 91. Part of that psalm says, "If you make the LORD your refuge, if you make the Most High your shelter, no evil will conquer you; no plague will come near your home. For he will order his angels to protect you wherever you go" (verses 9-11 NLT). The article recounted the adventures of soldiers during the World Wars, whole units of them, who prayed Psalm 91 every day. *Every one of them lived. I'm in a war right now with this blasted grizzly. I wonder if Psalm 91 will work for me?*

The sun slipped behind the mountain. Tall shadows crept between the tents. I gathered wood and built a campfire. In the flickering light I read Psalm 91 aloud, ending my prayer with, "Lord, please post Your angels around this camp to keep the grizzlies out." Darkness smothered the camp. A cool breeze whispered through, carrying the clean mountain air down from the peaks.

I hung a glowing lantern in the cook tent. Retreating to my guest tent, I lit the woodstove and tied Rye up. I slipped shells into the shotgun and chambered one. I thumbed cartridges into the .357 pistol and placed it on the cot next to my head by the bear spray and the flashlight. Instead of burrowing into my sleeping bag, I tucked it around my shoulders. I slipped on a black stocking cap so I could keep my head warm while listening for the bear. I rolled on my side, watched the dog, and waited.

The night lingered. A twig broke. I jerked up and reached for the flashlight. Then a couple deer bounced past. I knew if the deer were in camp, the bear wasn't. I lay back down. Just as I started to doze, an owl hooted. The sound floated eerily through the meadow. At midnight and at four I pulled my black jacket over my flannel pajamas and snuck into the cook tent to refuel the lantern. Finally the first rays of sunlight glistened through the canvas. The bear never showed.

The next terror-filled days were followed by sleepless nights. Even though I prayed while sitting by the campfire, I wondered, *Does Psalm 91 really work? Or has the bear left the country?* Every time a twig snapped or the wind rustled through the brush, I sat up and reached for the flashlight. I could barely keep my eyes open by the time I heard hoofbeats the fourth day.

I lumbered through the camp to watch the crew and guests ride through the grassy meadow. Darrin, pulling a string of mules, reined his horse over. He handed me the rope to the lead mule, dismounted, and asked, "Did you see any grizzlies? There are tracks *everywhere* around camp!"

I nonchalantly shook my head and replied, "Not a one." On the inside I was jumping up and down. *It worked! It really, really worked!* I didn't understand it, but reciting Psalm 91—seeking God's help—had kept the bears out of camp.

As time passed, each time I was in grizzly country and knew they were around, I talked to God, praying Psalm 91. I gained more confidence until I truly learned to "not be afraid of the terrors of the night" (verse 5). Now I pray Psalm 91 over my family and me each day. I might not be facing grizzlies, but I know when I pray God listens and protects us.

> *Lord, thank You for giving me Your Word, which goes forth to protect me from danger. Teach me to rest in Your promises. Amen.*

30

North Star

Jesus said to them, "Come with me!"
MATTHEW 4:19 CEV

Czar's hooves crunched through the snow, and the sound rippled through the forest. Only a sliver of moon hung in the dark-blue sky. When I exhaled, my breath hung in the air. Frosty air nipped my cheeks so I pulled the wool scarf over my nose. Today the temperature had dipped to 10 degrees below zero, and after sunset it continued to plummet. I felt as large as a snowman all bundled up in my wool Elmer Fudd hat, bulky wool mittens, winter parka, down vest, wool sweater, leather chaps, wool pants, long johns, and Sorel winter boots. But I was toasty warm. The air, crisp and clean. Over the years I'd learned to love riding alone at night. It gave me time to contemplate life. Tonight I had a 14-mile ride that would take four hours. I was heading to Monture Creek Camp to join the crew and guests who had gone out two days before.

I shifted my weight in the saddle and leaned forward to pat my Czar's bay-colored neck. It was so dark I couldn't see my arm or the outline of my horse. Leaning back in the saddle I gazed into the sky and commented, "God, what a gorgeous night." One by one the stars appeared. The Big Dipper twinkled into place, and then the Little Dipper. I stared at the North Star while my mind drifted back to an Old West lecture I'd heard. The instructor had told the story of the cattle drives that took place between the 1860s and 1880s.

In the still of the night, his cowboy-sounding drawl drifted through my memory.

> In those days 8 to 10 cowboys would ride out of Texas herding 2000 head of wild cows. That's not near enough guys to handle those wily, snorty critters. Most of those cowboys were 14- to 16-year-old boys, not even men by today's standards. They braved thousands of miles of wilderness filled with stampedes, flash floods, and Indians to deliver the herds to Montana. On the prairies, lightning struck the tallest thing around—cowboys wearing pistols who rode horses with metal shoes. There weren't any promises or guarantees. Their directions? Take a good bearing on the North Star the first night. Follow it for four months and you'll be there.

The North Star glimmered. I wondered, *What if clouds covered the sky the first week and they couldn't see the North Star? What if they had gone off-course just a couple of degrees those first few days? A thousand miles later they'd be off the map.* I shook my head. "God, I'm so glad You didn't say, 'Just ride off into them thar woods, and I'll be waiting for you—that is if you make it.'"

> *Lord, thank You for saying, "Come with me." I'm thrilled that You're with me every step of the way. Amen.*

31

Angels in the Snow

Praise the LORD! Praise the LORD from the heavens!
Praise him from the skies! Praise him, all his angels!…
Praise him, sun and moon! Praise him, all you twinkling stars!
Praise him, skies above!…Let every created thing give praise
to the LORD, for he issued his command,
and they came into being.

PSALM 148:1-5 NLT

Sunlight streamed into the tent. I squinted at my alarm clock. *Only eight thirty.* I'd only been asleep an hour. I groaned and rolled on my side. The steam from my breath floated in the air. It had snowed a few inches last night, and the brilliant sunlight glistened off the snow. It was like I had floodlights inside the tent. I jumped out of bed, grabbed a log, and threw it into the woodstove. Hopping back into bed, I pulled my red sleeping bag over my head to block the light. *I've got to get some sleep.* But in a few minutes the air under my sleeping bag grew stale, and I thought I was going to suffocate. I ripped the sleeping bag away from my face and tightly closed my eyes. I couldn't block out the light. The light had flipped my brain cells to "on." Like a computer, my thoughts chugged through my daily routine. I sighed. *Might as well get up. Another day of endless work...just like yesterday.*

Like a zombie I dressed and trudged through the snow to the cook tent. The black enamelware coffeepot simmered on the woodstove. *Maybe a little "go juice" will wake me up.* Grabbing my blue mug, I poured. The coffee was thick enough to float a horseshoe. I sat at the table and stared at the spiral notebook. Every day my "chore list" was at least a page long. I was the cook for this hunting tent camp. Late-season hunts were easy because the days were short, but this was September... with long hours of daylight. Because the best hunting was at dawn and dusk, I slept in split shifts. My alarm would beep at three o'clock so I could cook breakfast and send the hunters out the door before dawn. At seven thirty, after cleaning up dishes, I'd crawl back into my sleeping bag for another three hours of sleep. Once I awoke, I religiously stuck to my routine. In the evening everybody rode back into camp packing an enormous appetite. Oftentimes I didn't dry the last dish from dinner until ten. Then I'd plod down to the creek holding a flashlight, fill the water buckets and lug them up to the cook tent, and set the kitchen for breakfast. I was lucky if I crawled into my sleeping bag before eleven.

I glanced at the list: chop kindling, fuel lanterns, sweep guest tents, make fresh bread, bake pecan pies, and brush Czar. After shrugging into my wool jacket, I walked over to the woodpile, grabbed the axe, and chopped a pile of kindling. My back bowed as I carried heavy armloads of split wood and kindling to each guest tent and filled up the wood boxes in the cook tent.

Sweeping out the tents, I efficiently gathered the gas lanterns and took them to the work bench to refuel them. Robotically I trudged through the snow to the corral to collect the lanterns from the tack shed and to brush Czar. Grabbing a blue plastic curry comb, I pulled a halter off a hook. The wooden corral gate groaned as I slipped through. Czar lay basking in the warm sun that glinted off his reddish-brown coat. Fresh fluffy flakes of snow lay around him. Only his ears twitched and his eyes rolled as he watched me approach. I giggled. "Time to get up, you sleepyhead."

Czar stretched his legs and curled them toward his belly, sweeping the snow aside. I laughed. It reminded me of when I was a child. I'd lay flat on my back in the snow and sweep my arms and legs in a jumping-jack motion. When I stood up, the imprint in the snow looked like an angel.

Czar lazily rolled onto his back and wiggled. Then he flopped onto his side. It was almost as if he was purposely making a snow angel. He curled his legs underneath him, heaved to his feet, and shook off clumps of snow.

With delight I admired the horse angel. When Czar had flopped on his side, the imprint from his front legs smacking the ground almost looked like a trumpet. It appeared that the horse angel was blowing it. Momentarily I forgot my routine. The snow around me glittered in the sunlight like a sea of diamonds. Each flake shimmered multicolored rays of light: blues, greens, gold, and reds. I glanced around the pasture where all the horses had lain in the snow. Horse angels were everywhere, and they were all blowing trumpets! I could almost hear the regal notes. It was as if the angels were celebrating God's beauty of freshly fallen September snow.

I'd been so absorbed in my "get it done" routine that I'd almost missed it. Heaps of snowflakes stood on the wooden fence rails. A squirrel, sitting in a tree above me, scolded. His tail switched with every chirp, knocking piles of snow from the pine needles and onto my head. I laughed and brushed it out of my hair. I inhaled a deep breath of crisp air. On all sides of me the blue sky outlined glistening, snow-covered peaks. *How many times have I walked in and out of the cook tent doing chores and never noticed any of this? It's been here all along.*

I slipped the halter on Czar and gazed at the mountains while I brushed him. After putting him back in the corral, I gathered the lanterns. As I walked toward the cook tent I admired the way the snow clung to every twig on the bushes and the long stems of grass. *Lord,*

You sure went all out when You created this world. Thank You. Every moment I was outside the rest of the day, I gawked at God's creation. With a happy heart, my chores no longer seemed like drudgery. The day flew past. I even found myself humming as I washed dishes.

Lord, open my eyes to see the beauty You've placed around me,
especially when my days seem filled with drudgery. Amen.

32

Greener Pastures

*The Kingdom of Heaven is like a treasure that a man discovered
hidden in a field. In his excitement, he hid it again and
sold everything he owned to get enough money to buy the field.*

MATTHEW 13:44 NLT

My car's headlights pierced the night and the tires crunched
through the snow as I turned into my driveway. Groaning, I
stared at the snow banks that lined both sides of the drive and were
taller than my car. It was one o'clock in the morning. I'd just flown
in from Texas where I'd visited Sandy, a friend who was attending
Bible school. The last few days had been heavenly. The Texas sun had
warmed my bones, and the God-centered atmosphere had thawed my
heart. I'd gone to classes with her and watched the school put their
faith in action when Sandy took me to the mission where they volunteered their time and energy. The warehouse building had been filled
with homeless people who were being exposed to the light of God in
the workers' eyes and the hope found in Jesus in their voices. The stu-
dents were living in the kingdom of God. My heart longed to be in
an atmosphere like that.

Pulling up to the green metal gate, I hopped out and glanced across the pasture. Other than a few narrow paths the horses had created, the field was covered with a smooth four-foot-deep blanket of snow that glowed in the moonlight. I pushed open the gate. The headlights illuminated the horses on the other side of the electric fence. They were tromping through the snow to greet me. Dazzle, my black mare, tossed her head. Czar, my bay gelding, nickered. And my brown mule named Little Girl brayed.

I shouted, "Hi, guys! You won't believe what I brought home for you." Just before I left Texas, Sandy and I walked through knee-high grass at the mission. I got this crazy idea: Why not bring home a small trash bag of fresh grass for the horses? So I did.

I pulled the car forward and closed the gate behind me. Popping the hatch of the red station wagon, I unzipped my carry-on bag and pulled out the trash bag. Grabbing the bag and taking out a large wad of grass, I shuffled through the snow to the fence. When the critters smelled the "green," all three of their noses came up. They sniffed the air in disbelief. *Grass? Green grass in winter?* Quickly I doled a handful to Little Girl. She grabbed it and trotted away. Czar tossed his head, pinned his ears, and told her to scoot faster. I set the bag down, reached in with both hands, and held grass out to Czar and Dazzle. "You're only getting one handful each tonight. I don't want you to get sick because it's so rich."

They savored it. Green, slimy drool dripped out of their mouths. I yawned and said, "There will be more in the morning." I walked back to the car, jumped in, and drove the car down the road and into the garage. Too tired to carry the suitcase into the house, I went straight to bed. Snuggling under the covers, I was wrapped in the memories of the God-centered life at the mission. Before I was ready, the morning sun streamed into my bedroom. Yawning and stretching, I walked over to the window. Blue sky silhouetted the mountain peaks covered with snow. The sun made the snow in the pasture sparkle. Then I looked closer. Instead of a smooth blanket of snow in the pasture there were humps and bumps. I looked again, squinting, not believing my eyes. The field looked like it had been dug up with a backhoe. I frowned as I cast a glance from one end to the other. *What happened since last night?*

Then I saw my three critters huddled together in a corner of the field. They were digging through the snow like they were searching for buried treasure. As they pawed, the snow flew in heaps behind them. I gave out a deep belly laugh. *They're looking for more green grass! They must have thought I got it out of the pasture and figured where there was some, there must be more.* They'd spent the entire night looking for it. There was barely a spot they'd missed. As I smiled I heard deep within my spirit, "If you will dig into My Word like they have the pasture, you'll create a God-centered atmosphere in your heart. That's where it begins—within you."

I pressed my nose against the window, watching Czar push his muzzle along the ground, searching for something green. *Lord, I am hungry for You, just like they're hungry for fresh grass.* I walked into the kitchen and turned on the coffee. Snuggling into my rocker, I opened my Bible to read for a while.

> *Lord, Thank You for showing me that I don't need to go someplace else to experience You. Instead, I need to immerse myself in Your Word and You, the living Force that fills my life with hope, peace, love, and joy. Amen.*

33

Blind Colt

The LORD God gives me the right words
to encourage the weary.

ISAIAH 50:4 CEV

Frost coated every blade of the tall grass, glittering blues and greens in the morning light. It was one of my favorite times of year—May. The snow had melted out of the valley, the robins had returned, and yesterday one of my mares had given birth to a most precious colt that I'd named Obadiah. The weathered wooden barn door creaked as I slipped into the stall carrying a flake of alfalfa hay. The bay mare, Snipe, nickered. Prancing, Obadiah shook his head at me as if to say, "It's about time you came to visit!"

I dropped the hay into the wooden feeder. Snipe stuffed her mouth as if she hadn't eaten in days. I ruffled the colt's red-velveteen coat and its short curly black mane. I patted Snipe's neck. "It's tough feeding that baby, isn't it?" The colt turned toward me, cocking his head side to side. His long, black eyelashes rimmed beautiful brown eyes. The colt's steamy breath escaped his dainty nostrils and formed droplets on his black whiskers.

The colt charged his mom's udder. His muzzle wrinkled as he pushed into it. He slurped and tugged, butted a bit and slurped some more. He switched his curly black tail, stomped his front foot, and turned toward me with milk dripping down his chin.

I scratched Snipe's shoulder. "What a beautiful healthy boy you have."

Obadiah cocked his head, listening to me. He switched his tail and whirled.

I watched in horror as he ran headlong into the wall.

He bounced backward and shook his head.

I blinked. *What's going on?*

Obadiah cocked his head as if examining the wall. Once again, he bounded forward and charged into the wall. He lost his balance and crumpled to the ground.

Shocked, I gaped at the piled-up and panting colt. *Can horses be mentally retarded?* I wondered.

Snipe nickered to him, asking, "Are you okay?"

Obadiah gathered his legs and lurched to his feet. He nickered an answer.

His mom sniffed his nose. Tenderly she brushed her muzzle across the top of his back and down his legs, checking him over.

Obadiah bumped his mouth along her belly until he hit her udder. Fiercely he latched hold and sucked.

I chewed on my lip. *Was that a freak accident? No, Snipe is acting weird too. She's treating him like he's fragile.*

Obadiah sucked and tugged. He turned loose, letting the teat snap. Slurping milk, he pranced around his mother. Suddenly he spun and ran smack dab into another wall.

It's almost like he didn't see it. I walked over to his side. *Is he blind?* Wrapping my right arm over his neck, I snuggled him next to the right side of my body. With my left hand a few feet in front of his face, I slowly waved. His eyes didn't follow the movement.

I sighed deeply. Pointing my finger, I moved it toward his left eye, inching it closer and closer until I nearly touched his eyeball. He didn't blink. My heart cried, *Lord, he can't be blind. He looks perfectly healthy.* His warm body leaned against me. I waved my hand in front of his right eye. Nothing.

Aghast, I wondered, *How can I keep a blind horse?* My mind chugged through the facts. I couldn't turn him out with the herd because the pastures were hundreds of acres of rolling hills, streams, and cliffs. If he got scared and took off running, he might run full-blast into a barbed-wire fence. Or worse yet, he might go over a cliff. I had no way to keep him in a stall because I went into the mountains for weeks at a time for my job. My heart shattered. The horse market was horrible. Even good horses were killed these days because no one wanted them. I knew I'd never find a home for a blind horse. *If he's blind I don't have a choice. I have to put him down…and do it before I get too attached.* "But it's already too late for that," I murmured.

Tears welled up in my eyes. Snipe nuzzled the white star on Obadiah's forehead. He was her fourth colt—the third since I'd owned her. I'd been heartbroken when I found out about her first colt. Before I bought her, she'd given birth to an "oops" baby. The owners immediately took it away and killed it because they didn't want the hassle. Months later, when I bought her, she was still grieving. *I don't know if I can do that to her. Lord, I need Your wisdom and direction.*

All night long that colt drifted in and out of my dreams. The next day I rubbed my eyes as I leaned against the exam room counter in the vet clinic. Snipe stood tied to the cinderblock wall, pawing impatiently. Dr. Roulette held the stethoscope to Obadiah's ribs. "He's a healthy little guy in almost every way. But I'm afraid you're right. He is blind."

My tears blurred the room. I rubbed my forehead and looked at my boots.

"If you want, I'll put him down." Dr. Roulette caressed the colt's soft fur. Obadiah nibbled on Dr. Roulette's blue shirt and then grabbed a button and sucked. Dr. Roulette chuckled and pulled out the shirt.

Softly he said, "There might be an option. It's a long shot. I just heard about a veterinary school that has done some research on blindness in colts. I can give them a call. Maybe there's something we can do. It might take a few days to get an answer." He rubbed Obadiah's neck. "You don't have anything to lose by waiting. If there isn't any hope, we can put him down then."

Obadiah nickered to his mom. Snipe swung her head and replied. She pulled on the rope to get free.

Dr. Roulette's words sparked a glimmer of hope in my heart. I nodded. *I have to give it a try.* "Let me know."

I drove the stock truck home and led Snipe and Obadiah into the stall. It was the safest place to keep Obadiah while I waited for the phone to ring. On the second day, Dr. Roulette called with a question, "Do you know the exact date Snipe was bred?"

I twisted the phone cord. "I'm not sure. I left all the mares at the breeders for two cycles. They were pasture bred. I can find out though." I hung up, called the breeder, and then called the vet back.

I told him the information, and he excitedly said, "Yes! That means the colt was born two-and-a-half, maybe three weeks early." He explained that the studies have found that often when colts are premature, their eyes aren't totally developed. But they usually continue to develop during the weeks after the birth. "Can you bring him back to the clinic in two weeks?"

I breathed a sigh of relief. "Yes!"

The days dragged past. Every hour I slipped into the stall and waved my hand in front of Obadiah's long eyelashes, waiting for some kind of response. Four days later he shifted his head as if he could see shadows. A week later he blinked when my finger almost touched his eye.

Two weeks later I stood in the clinic holding Obadiah's lead rope while Dr. Roulette shined a flashlight into the colt's eyes. When he was done testing, a grin slid across his face. "His eyes are normal! He can see just fine."

I jumped up and down. "Yes, yes, yes!"

Obadiah snorted and hauled back on the lead rope.

I was filled with joy as I watched him stand with all four feet braced as he leaned away from the rope. I slowly reached to pet him. He examined my hand, his nostrils flaring. I touched the side of his stiff neck. As I rubbed him, he melted with relief and leaned into my hand. I looked at the doctor. "Thank you for encouraging me to wait. You saved this little guy's life."

Lord, thank You for friends who encourage me when I'm in the dark hours of life. Help me become a person who speaks words of encouragement to people when they face difficulties. Amen.

34

Donkey Honk

After [the interview with King Herod], the wise men went their way.
And the star they had seen in the east guided them to Bethlehem.
It went ahead of them and stopped over the place where the child was.

MATTHEW 2:9 NLT

Mel recited the bloodlines of his prized mares that were with foal. As I listened, I leaned back in the dining room chair and stirred cream into my coffee. I'd driven to Mel's ranch in North Dakota to see his breeding operation. He owned a simple, old, white farmhouse with a few outbuildings in the middle of a prairie. Mel pulled registration papers out of a manila envelope. As he spread them out on the table, he rubbed his leathery face with his callused hand. He pointed at a paper. "Wait till you see this one's colt. It's a dandy. He was just born yesterday, and I watched the whole thing."

Astonished, I leaned forward. "You were there? You actually saw him born?"

"Of course. I watch all my mares give birth."

I sipped my steaming coffee. *How can that be?* The breeders I knew *wanted* to watch their colts be born, but somehow the mares eluded them and gave birth without being under their watchful eyes. Setting down my cup, I asked, "So how do you do it? Do you set your alarm every hour when the mares are due? And then get up and look at them through a high-tech video camera that's set up in their stalls?"

Mel grinned and said, "Nope. I don't have a video camera, and I don't miss a lick of sleep."

I sat back and crossed my arms.

Mel's green eyes twinkled. "I've got a secret. And if you're nice, I just might tell you. Bundle up. Let's go meet the critters."

I pulled on my wool gloves and zipped my brown Carhartt jacket as I trudged behind Mel to the makeshift corrals that separated the mares with foals from the rest of the herd. One corral held a lone horse standing close to the fence. April snowflakes lazily drifted from the gray sky as my friend reached through the fence and patted a flashy chestnut stud with white socks. "This is the gentlest giant you'll ever meet. And he's the daddy to all these." Mel waved his arm toward a half-a-dozen good-looking foals.

I glanced at the gangly foals that stood by their mothers' sides. They stretched their necks and curiously watched our every move. "Were you able to watch any of these being born?"

A grin slithered across Mel's face. "Every single one," he replied.

I scratched the back of my neck. I'd never heard of a breeder being able to watch *every* colt being born. *Is Mel pulling my leg?*

The rancher chuckled. "C'mon and meet my secret." He turned and walked toward a small shed. I shrugged and followed. As soon as we rounded the corner, a donkey scuttled over to the fence and brayed. It brayed and brayed, on and on, as if saying, "Gosh, I thought you'd never come over here to visit me!" Snowflakes clung to the long eyelashes of the short, shaggy critter as she belted out another song.

A newborn colt and its mother stood under the lean-to shed in the same paddock as the donkey. I looked at them with alarm. Tidbits I'd been taught about donkeys and mules swirled through my mind. Donkeys and mules generally hate small animals and purposely kill them—or so I'd heard. I'd seen mules with the look of blood in their eyes as they took out after unfamiliar dogs. I'd been warned to never let them near colts because they'd do the same thing to them.

Mel slipped the chain off the gate and motioned for me to squeeze through. He closed the gate behind us. The donkey walked over to the colt and nuzzled it. Then that cute beast looked at us as if to ask, "Isn't he fine?"

Confused, I glanced at the mare that was casually munching hay. *How strange. Usually a mare has a fit if anything or anyone gets close to her colt.* But she didn't seem to care in the least. She almost looked relieved.

Mel ruffled the long, tan coat of the donkey. "Here's my secret. This donkey is worth its weight in gold." Mel scratched the side of her neck. The donkey leaned into his fingers as Mel told me the story. Two years ago he went to a BLM auction for wild horses and donkeys. As the auctioneer's voice rang out, there was one shaggy little donkey nobody bid on. Mel had no reason to raise his hand, but his heart went out to that critter as it stood in the ring shivering with fear. Up went Mel's number. After loading that poor little donkey into his horse trailer, he wondered what on earth he'd just done. He too had heard about a donkey's aggressive behavior toward small animals. He knew he had to keep the donkey separate from the newborn colts.

As the seasons changed and the colts grew, he finally turned the donkey loose with the mares and colts. He kept a close eye on the donkey, noticing that she spent all her time with the colts. She'd groom them and babysit while the mothers enjoyed afternoon naps in the sun. When the next spring rolled around, he had several mares due to foal. He wasn't looking forward to setting his alarm every hour all night long so he could check on them in case they had problems with the births.

One night he was pretty sure a mare was going to foal. When he crawled into bed, he set his alarm to go off in an hour. Each hour he woke up, grabbed his flashlight, and walked down to the paddock to check on her. In the wee hours of the morning, he crawled back into bed and drifted off to sleep. He awoke with a start. That little donkey was bellowing and braying. Disgustedly, he rolled over, wishing the donkey would be quiet. But it went on and on, louder and longer. Finally thinking something was wrong with the beast, Mel pulled on his boots, shrugged into his jacket, grabbed a flashlight, and trudged through the pasture. The donkey was still braying and braying. Mel shone the beam of his flashlight toward the little animal. Its head was shoved way over the rail of the mare's paddock. Mel directed the beam into the mare's paddock. In the lean-to shed the mare was lying down and straining. Her water had broken, and she was in full labor. A little hoof poked out. Mel watched in awe as he witnessed his first birth.

Mel smiled at me as he brushed the snowflakes off the donkey. "I would have missed that birth if it hadn't been for this little gal. That mare had waited for me to go back into the house before she lay down to have the colt." Mel chuckled and scratched the donkey. "My secret weapon announces every baby's birth. I quit setting an alarm a long time ago. Instead I've trained my ear to listen for her braying. Funny thing is, the neighbors don't hear her. It doesn't take much time for me to slip on my boots these days when I hear her."

I looked at the snow gently falling on the donkey's tan coat and into the makeshift stable. I was reminded of something I'd read about—a scene some 2000 years ago, when in a manger in Bethlehem a child was born. People who saw the star and read the prophecies and the ones who heard the chorus of angels signaling the Messiah's birth went to see the newborn. But others who saw and heard the same signs missed the greatest event in history because they hadn't developed a relationship with God.

I scratched the donkey's neck as I thought, *Jesus is coming back soon, and I don't want to miss the next greatest event in history.*

Lord, I'm hungry for a deeper relationship with You. Help me recognize the signs of Your return. Amen.

35

In Step

God has combined the members of the body...so that there
should be no division in the body, but that its parts
should have equal concern for each other.

1 CORINTHIANS 12:24-25

The first rays of the sun rose over the mountain peak at the Benchmark Trailhead outside of Augusta, Montana. Trucks and horse trailers formed a line between the rows of wooden corrals. This trailhead was a four-hour drive from the ranch where I worked. We'd hauled all the guests, gear, horses, and mules over yesterday afternoon, and we'd camped out so we could get an early start this morning. Both the first-scheduled summer trip and the second-scheduled trip were leaving from here. Today more than 35 people—crew and guests— bustled full-speed ahead. The corrals brimmed with more than 60 head of horses and mules that were trotting around and stirring up clouds of dust. Wranglers caught and saddled the stock. My boss and I fried bacon and made coffee on wood cookstoves. The guests stuffed their sleeping bags, closed their duffels, and then lined up with plates in hand.

After Karen and I flipped pancakes and cooked eggs for the guests, the crew wandered over. Darrin ran his hand through his sandy-blond hair. "I'll take four pancakes and three eggs over medium." I nodded and cracked the eggs on the edge of the cast iron griddle.

I glanced at Farmer, the new guy on crew. He stood about six feet tall and was built like a brick. Rubbing his black moustache he said, "Same."

Brett, a tall, drink-of-water wrangler, walked up behind Farmer and slapped him on his back. Chuckling, Brett pointed to Darrin and said, "Don't listen to anything that guy tells you. He's *second* schedule."

Darrin rolled his eyes. "He's going to be with me the next 10 days, so who else is he going to listen to?" He smiled at Farmer. "Don't worry. Second schedule has more fun."

Brett strolled over to Karen. "Five pancakes, four eggs, and can I get a couple extra strips of bacon?"

Smiling, Karen wrapped a gray strand of hair behind her ear and nodded.

Brett walked back and, while looking at Farmer, playfully slapped Darrin in the stomach. "We eat better on first schedule."

I picked up the metal spatula and waved it at him. "Hey, watch your mouth!" Leaning toward Farmer I whispered, "Bill's the best boss in the world. And he's *our* boss."

Poor Farmer was caught in the middle of a fierce rivalry that had gone on for years. Sometimes the comments were funny; other times they tended to be brash.

Later Brett laid out mantie tarps on the ground and taught Farmer how to build a load of sleeping bags and gear. The whole time Brett bragged about the incredible places in the high country, such as Diamond Lakes, where he was going because he was on *first* schedule.

When Darrin showed Farmer how to sling the packs on a mule, he said, "We boogie down the trail on *our* schedule."

When all was ready, the guests swung into their saddles and rode into the wilderness with Bill in the lead. I looked at the crews still working and waved my arm toward the mules. "Let's see which schedule can get the mules packed the fastest." Brett and Darrin spun into action while Farmer uncomfortably leaned against the wood corral, staying out of the way of the two cyclones. When they were finished, Brett and Darrin raced to tie their mules together. Brett hopped in the saddle and headed down the trail. Darrin, with his string, was hot on his tail. By the time Farmer stepped into his saddle, his eyes were glazed over. I'm sure his head was spinning. I slipped into the saddle and fell in line.

The trail wound through the forest. The sound of the horses and mules stepping down the dirt trail reminded me of drumbeats. I glanced ahead at Brett's string. The mules, walking single file behind him, were all walking in step. Right, left, right, left. I grinned when I noticed that their long ears flopped in step too. First the right was forward and as it slapped backward, the left snapped forward—all in sync with their feet.

Darrin's sorrel horse followed behind Brett's last mule—and those two were in step. Puzzled, I glanced down the line. Each of Darrin's mules was in step, along with their ears. *Every animal is synchronized from the top of their ears to the bottom of their hooves. Two strings of mules that carried gear for two separate trips, with different destinations, were working in step while they were together.* I glanced at Farmer, who sat quietly in his saddle while enjoying the terrain. *Those mules are showing Farmer a better job of teamwork than I did.* I gathered my reins. *I shouldn't have egged the boys on. I could have ended the banter and welcomed Farmer as part of the entire team.*

During the next few days while riding the trail, I focused on making friends with the new guy. In the evenings I taught him how to become a working, contributing member of our crew.

> *Lord, thank You for giving us fun times to banter and compete, but let me know when it's time to speak and act as a team. Amen.*

36

Friends

A man of many companions may come to ruin,
but there is a friend who sticks closer than a brother.

PROVERBS 18:24

I huffed and puffed as I jogged up the grassy hill and into the log lodge at Lake Upsata Guest Ranch. I was working there as a cook. *Ecstatic* didn't even come close to describing how I felt. My mare had just given birth to the cutest, red, floppy-eared mule whom I'd dubbed Wind Dancer. I needed to call the vet, but I was rushing because my animals were in a pasture that sloped into the lake. I was worried about the foal falling in and drowning. I raced through the dining room and into the office, picked up the phone, and punched in the numbers. When Dr. Brown came on the line he said, "I'll be at the ranch in an hour. By chance, did you check the placenta?"

I hesitated for a minute. *Where was the placenta?* In my excitement I hadn't thought of looking for it. Besides, Wind Dancer had surprised me. I'd planned on moving the mare into a small and safer pasture before giving birth. But Wind Dancer had arrived three weeks early when the mare had been grazing in the enormous grassy meadow with her "boyfriend," my 26-year-old Czar. I twisted the phone cord. "No, I didn't see it."

"I'd like to take a look at it. Do you think you can find it?"

"Sure." I hung up the phone. *I've got to call Dena and share the news.*

Dena's voice bubbled. "Congratulations! Krystal and I'll jump into the truck and be down in a few minutes."

I couldn't wait to show Dena the baby. That past winter I'd gone through a personal life crisis, and Dena had been my emotional support. She was always encouraging me, forbidding me to speak negative thoughts, and reminding me to look for the good in every situation.

I skipped down the lodge steps. My tennis shoes crunched on the gravel as I jogged down the long road to the pasture. When I topped the hill and slid between the wooden rails, I noticed Czar was grazing next to the lake. The sun glistened off his bay coat. The sorrel mare stood 100 feet away, slowly pulling up a few stalks of grass and chewing them. She rested one of her hind legs. She looked exhausted from the labor. Wind Dancer was racing laps around her mother. With her elbows and knees wobbling, she spun and scampered toward the lake.

I cringed and held my breath. *Stop!*

Wind Dancer pinned back her ears. Lacking coordination, she ran helter-skelter down the hill.

Czar's head popped up. As the foal roared down the grassy slope, he shook his head and then trotted across the field until he was in front of where she would be soon.

She skidded to a stop just before running into him.

I watched in fascination as Czar nudged her with his nose, pushing her back uphill and away from the lake. He gently herded her a few more steps. When Wind Dancer caught sight of her mom, she whinnied and scrambled up the hill on her own. Leaning against her mom, she tucked her head under her mom's belly, butted the udder, and sucked.

I breathed a sigh of relief as I hiked down the hill toward Czar.

On a small flat spot I saw the placenta. As I walked closer, I noticed that instead of being a nice neat package, it was torn to shreds, and the ground around it was smeared with blood. I stared in shock. The coyotes had already drug it around and chewed on it. *Thank You, God, that they didn't kill Wind Dancer.* I knew there was only one reason why they hadn't finished eating it. Czar had chased them off.

Every day I prayed for God to protect my animals and me. He had used Czar to protect Wind Dancer from the craftiness of the coyotes and the dangers of the lake. I walked to Czar and scratched the white star on his forehead. "You're a one-in-a-million friend."

Dena's Dodge diesel rumbled onto the gravel road. Czar moved his head up and down as I continued to scratch. "Dena's a one-in-a-million friend too," I added. My negative thoughts and words had been just as dangerous to me as the lake and the coyotes were to Wind Dancer. I could have drowned in the depths of despair and been consumed by negativity. But Dena helped protect me.

The truck turned into the driveway. I waved and hurried up to the pickup. Dena and her daughter Krystal jumped out, slammed the doors, and slipped through the wooden rails. Krystal squealed with delight as she scampered to Wind Dancer's side. Krystal scratched the foal's neck while Dena scratched the white star on her forehead. "Oh Rebecca, she's beautiful."

I grinned. "She's awesome. And thanks for all your help over the last year."

When the vet arrived, he gave the mare and Wind Dancer clean bills of health and confirmed my suspicions that the placenta had been chewed by coyotes.

> *Lord, thank You for giving me friends who protect me when I'm weak and vulnerable. Teach me how to protect others through the gift of friendship. Amen.*

37

Salt

You are the salt of the earth. But if the salt loses its saltiness,
how can it be made salty again? It is no longer good for anything,
except to be thrown out and trampled by men.

MATTHEW 5:13

Amarillo, the copper-colored gelding I was riding, picked his way down the rutted trail through the lodgepole pines. Nine mules slogged along behind us. The mud was so deep that each time they lifted a hoof it slurped out of the mud. It had been a long day. In the morning I'd stacked bales of hay on the truck, hauled them to the end of the road, unloaded and mantied them, and then loaded each mule with two bales, one on each side. I glanced at my watch. Five o'clock...and I was 14 miles down the trail. A cool breeze rustled the trees. Rain dripped from the brim of my cowboy hat, ran down my slicker, soaked my jeans, and meandered into my boots. I shivered with cold and wiggled my wet toes, trying to warm them.

At the fork in the trail I turned toward Monture Camp, anticipating sitting in a chair next to the wood cookstove, pulling off my boots, and warming my toes. But as Amarillo's hooves clopped into camp, I saw the fluorescent-orange cook tarp sagging. It was filled with rainwater—ready to collapse and soak the kitchen supplies stored underneath. The crew hadn't stretched it tight enough when they'd pitched the tent. I groaned. *Don't they have any common sense?* I wondered. This season I was working with a new group. From the looks of the tarp, they were a bunch of greenhorns with no sense. *It's going to be a long year.*

I pulled off my leather gloves, wrung the rainwater out of them, and tucked them under my belt as I glanced around camp. Nobody was in sight. *They must be cutting rails.* I tied Amarillo and the mules to the hitching rack, and then I hustled over to the tarp to dump the rainwater. Dirty pots littered the table and kitchen boxes. *What a bunch of slobs. Don't they know this'll bring in bears?*

Then I glanced at the wood stacked next to the cookstove. Every stick was green and in big chunks. *Don't they have enough sense to cut dry wood—and to split them into small enough wedges so it will burn hot?* I pulled off my hat and slapped it against my slicker to shed the rain. As I slipped it back on, out of the corner of my eye I saw something tan lying on the ground. I walked over and nudged it with the toe of my boot. *Oh great.* It was an ax head with the shredded remains of a handle attached. A porcupine had gnawed it. *Why didn't they hang this up after they used it? Don't they know that the porcupines are hungry for salt, and the salty sweat from our hands penetrates the wood handle?*

I seethed as I slogged through the mud and unsaddled Amarillo. The hair on the back of my neck stood up. I felt like I was being watched. Turning, I saw a deer with a glove flopping out of the corner of her mouth. *She's chewing it for the salt,* I thought. Quickly I looked at my belt—only one glove! The other had obviously fallen off somewhere.

I hollered, "Hey! That's my glove." The doe batted her long eyelashes. The glove flopped as she continued to chew enthusiastically.

"Drop that glove!" I commanded.

She tilted her head side to side and wiggled her long, tan ears.

I ran toward her.

Momentarily she froze, and then she bounded through the pines, the glove clenched between her teeth.

I bolted after her, dodging trees and jumping logs.

She bounced 100 yards ahead, stopped, turned toward me, and chewed that glove like it was her last meal.

I stood still, watching her. *It didn't take much salt to lure her into camp.* I frowned. *Or much on the ax handle to draw in the porcupine.* A Bible verse drifted through my mind, something about believers being the salt of the earth. *Ah, I get it. The salt is the thoughts we store in our hearts. Not only do they preserve us, but they draw other people to us. People are salt hungry too. Hungry for the salt of God.*

The doe rolled the glove around in her mouth. My mind drifted. *Salt in her mouth. Gosh, I don't have any salt in my mouth...or in my thoughts.* All I had dwelt on since I'd ridden into camp was what a bunch of idiots I was going to be working with. I sighed. *Maybe they didn't have much outdoors sense, but that didn't make them stupid. Nobody had taught them what they needed to know out here. But I can.* I chewed on my lip. *Okay, God, I'll show them Your salt by patiently teaching them the ropes. And I'm going to start with the kitchen tarp.*

The doe tipped her head while she stared at me. I clapped my hands and shouted, "Drop it!" She finally spit out the glove and took off. I ran over and snatched it off the ground. As I pulled it on I realized two of the fingers now had holes in them. I wiggled my fingertips, watching them through the tooth-chewed gaps. *This is a good reminder that a little salt goes a long way.*

> *Lord, thank You for reminding me to season my conversations with salt—the fruit of Your Spirit—to draw people to You. Amen.*

38

Late

Each one shall bear his own load.

GALATIANS 6:5

A hint of light from the rising sun poked through the flap on my tent. I rubbed my eyes and rolled over in my sleeping bag as my mind drifted slowly into reality. *Oh no!* I sat up and grabbed for my pocket alarm clock. It glowed 5:30. I was an hour late! I examined the switch. The alarm was still set, but it had never gone off. I was the cook on a summer pack trip, and normally by now I'd be dressed, have my duffel packed, my sleeping bag stuffed in its bag, my tent down, and everything hauled over to the makeshift kitchen. There I'd have a fire lit in the stove and the coffee would be boiling, ready for the wranglers when they herded in the horses.

And worse yet, I was working with a new guy on crew—Doug. He was from the Northern Territories of Canada and had lots of back-country experience. I was looking forward to having him on our team. I groaned. *I slept in late. What kind of first impression am I going to make now?*

I reached for my glasses. I didn't feel them. Frantically I patted around the top of my sleeping bag. Nothing. *I must have moved them in my sleep.* I reached for my flashlight and flicked the switch. Nothing again. The batteries were dead. *Without glasses or contacts I can't see to cook. And how am I going to get my contacts in without a flashlight?* I shook my head, reached for the contact case, opened it, and carefully cradled a contact on the tip of my finger. Holding my eyelid open, I stuck it in and blinked. *Not bad. Now for the next one.* But when I snapped the left contact on my eye, a piece of dirt was lodged underneath it. "Ow!" I ripped the contact out and wondered, *Is there anything else that can go wrong to slow me down?* After rinsing the contact with saline solution, I slid it in and blinked.

I reached into my green duffel bag and pulled out my riding clothes. Negative thoughts assaulted my mind. *Good going, Rebecca. You've got a 20-mile horseback ride ahead of you today, and by getting up late you're going to make everyone late. Great team member you are.* Quickly I dressed and got busy. I organized my morning: first light the fire in the cookstove, haul 20 gallons of water from the creek, put the bacon on the griddle to fry, make sack lunches, pour pancake batter on the griddle for the guests as they come in for breakfast, haul another 20 gallons of water, wash and dry the stack of dirty dishes, pack all the dishes and food... In my mind, the morning snowballed out of control. I should have set my second alarm as a backup. *What kind of team member am I?*

A cool breeze rustled the flap on my tent as I hastily stuffed my sleeping bag and packed my duffel. I found my glasses shoved in a corner. I pulled on work boots but didn't bother to lace them. I just tucked the laces into the tops. After tearing down the tent, I piled my arms with my duffel bag, sleeping bag, and the tent. Under the load, I wobbled over to the tree where we stacked the duffels to be packed on the mules. With tunnel vision, I jogged over to the kitchen tarp and stopped in shock. The wood cookstove belched smoke. Doug was walking up the hill carrying two buckets of water. Coffee boiled in the blue enamelware coffeepot. *Oh God, thank You for sending me help!*

Doug smiled as he set down the buckets with a slosh. "Morning. I figured you could use a hand," he said.

I nodded. "My alarm didn't go off. I guess you didn't go with the wranglers."

Doug shook his head. "They didn't need me, but it looks like you did."

Picking up the coffeepot, I poured a cup and handed it to Doug. "You're right. Thanks." I poured a cup for myself, and we each pulled a camp stool next to the wood stove. Only a few minutes ago I was focused on what a rotten team member I was. But I hadn't been late on purpose, and sometimes unexpected things happen. I leaned back in my chair and sipped the steaming brew. *What is a team? It's being synchronized with other members so that the tasks come together easily.* Over the years I'd done that many times for others, and this morning Doug had done that for me. *It's about giving and receiving,* floated through my mind. *Doug didn't look down on me. No, instead he felt blessed to be able to chip in and help. And I was glad to receive.*

Lord, I love being part of Your team by giving my life to You and receiving Your precious promises. Thank You. Amen.

39

Porcupine Muzzle

*When you do a charitable deed, do not let your left hand know
what your right hand is doing, that your charitable deed may
be in secret; and your Father who sees in secret
will Himself reward you openly.*

MATTHEW 6:3-4

Twenty head of horses and mules stood in the large corral. I buttoned my tan, wool jacket to shut out the cool morning breeze. After slipping a brown halter over my shoulder, I tucked it next to my body so the horses and mules wouldn't see it. They knew a halter meant getting caught and being put to work—and usually all of them wanted the day off. But today I wasn't catching stock to put them to work.

The tall, old gate creaked as I slid through. The horses and mules circled around me, begging for scratches. That is...all except Gruella. I stood on my tiptoes to look over the crowd. The handsome blue-gray horse with the black mane, tail, and legs stood against the rail with his head high, his eyes wide, his nostrils flared. A couple dozen porcupine quills stuck out of his muzzle. *How am I going to catch him and pull out those quills by myself? He's in pain, it's going to hurt when*

I pull them out, and getting a rope on him without hitting the quills will be difficult.

I'd discovered the horse's plight this morning when I went out to the pasture to catch my saddle horse. I'd noticed Gruella was hanging back from the herd. I walked out to check on him. Seeing the quills sticking like white whiskers out of his dark gray muzzle made me cringe. Not only did they probably hurt, but he couldn't eat or drink with them embedded in his sensitive nose. I stepped closer. He ducked his head and turned away. As soon as I got within 15 feet of him, he evaded me. I stood still and gathered my thoughts. Porcupine quills have a fishhook barblike tip. Once embedded, they only move one direction naturally—deeper into the flesh. I'd heard stories about quills that worked their way into an animal's brain, killing it. I knew I needed to pull the quills out as quickly as possible. After glancing around the gently rolling, grassy hills of the 500-acre pasture I decided what to do. Instead of chasing him, I caught and saddled my bay gelding, rounded up the whole herd, and pushed them into the round corral.

Now dust clouds billowed from the horses' hooves as they milled around me. I scratched the rear of a sorrel mare as I squeezed past her and nonchalantly edged toward Gruella. The horses and mules mobbed me as I ambled across the corral. When I got within 10 feet of him, Gruella squealed and ran to the other side, holding his head high so nothing would bump against the quills that were obviously inflicting a lot of pain. *He's not going to let me near him.*

I stepped up on a wooden rail and looked at those quills. *If I do get close, how can I catch him? He's not going to let me put the halter over them.* The only way to catch him was by tossing a rope over his head. With the quills doing their work, I knew that would be nearly impossible. He was going to dodge anything that got close to his face. I moaned. *It figures that I'm the only person at the ranch today.* Every other crew member was on a pack trip and not expected home for days. *Who else can I get to help?* The ranch community of Ovando, Montana, was only a couple minutes drive away. Town consisted of a post office and a general store/gas station. Only a handful of folks lived there. Usually during the day nobody was on the street; everyone was working on ranches or in the woods. But it was my only hope. *Lord, please have someone in town who can rope and is willing to help.*

I left the corral, went to my room, grabbed my keys, and then hopped into the pickup and drove the dusty road to town. When I parked in front of the hitching rack at the store, Peggy was sitting on the porch with Howard Copenhaver. Only his white hair told of his 70-plus years. Howard was as fit-as-a-fiddle and still worked full-time as an outfitter and guide. His wispy five-foot-eight frame couldn't have weighed 120 pounds soaking wet, even if he was wearing all his clothes, chaps, and boots. But he was made of steel. He'd been raised on a ranch, cowboyed, and worked hard his whole life.

I jumped out of the truck and tipped my cowboy hat. "Howard, what are you doing here? I thought you'd be in the hills."

The man leaned back in the chair. His straw cowboy hat was tipped back on his head and a cigarette hung out of the corner of his mouth. His voice was graveled. "Everyone else went out today, but I had some things to catch up on. I'm leaving in the morning."

Peggy looked at my pale face and patted the chair next to her. "Everything okay?" she asked.

I shook my head and said, "Nope." Then I curled up in the chair and shared my story.

Howard asked, "Where did you say he was?"

Peggy looked at Howard, chuckled, and slapped him on the knee. "What are you doing just sitting here?"

Howard grinned and nodded.

Soon a cloud of dust boiled behind my gold-and-white pickup as I pulled next to the corral. Jumping out, I grabbed a pair of pliers from behind the seat and slipped them in my back pocket. I also grabbed a bottle of rubbing alcohol. Howard's pickup bumped over the gravel road and parked next to mine. He stepped out with his well-worn lariat coiled in his hand.

He walked over to the corral and immediately built a loop. He held it in his right hand, letting the loop drape by his side. The horses and mules that were roaming around in the corral stopped, their eyes fastened on him. Gruella's eyes were wide with the whites showing. The wooden gate creaked as I opened it a sliver for Howard to slip through. I closed it after him, and then leaned my arms over the top rail and watched.

Gruella stood on the far side of the corral, his nostrils flared, his senses alert. With each breath, the quills fluttered. He turned and faced Howard. The horses and mules milled between them.

Looking at his worn cowboy boots, Howard held the lariat close to his body, coiled and ready. He took two steps and then stopped. The herd slowly drifted away from him, eventually leaving a clearing between Gruella and Howard.

The gelding nervously stared at him and then at the herd that was drifting away. He quickly stepped toward the other animals.

I barely saw Howard's right arm flick upward. The rope sang. In awe I watched it gracefully float over Gruella's head and settle around his shoulders. The blue-gray horse snorted and sat on his haunches, tightening the rope. Before I could blink, Howard had slipped the rope around Gruella's legs and swept him off his feet. Gruella hit the ground with a thud. Before he could struggle up, Howard tossed a couple loops of the lariat around his feet, effectively tying him up.

I hustled through the gate, pulling the pliers out of my back pocket. I handed them to the old cowhand.

"How did you do that?" I asked. "You didn't even swing the rope."

I sat on Gruella's neck to hold him down while Howard quickly plucked out quills.

A grin slid across Howard's leathery face. "A lot of practice." He pinched another quill with the pliers and gave a strong pull. Gruella groaned in pain. Compassion flooded the cowboy's face. "You see, I only had one easy chance. This horse is in pain. If he'd a-seen me swinging the rope over my head, he would've been braced and waiting.

He probably would have dodged the loop and got riled up. Then it would've taken a long time to calm him down so we could catch him." Howard winced as he yanked out another quill. Blood dotted Gruella's muzzle. "I built my loop while I was still outside the corral. Sometimes it's better to do things when nobody's watching." Howard yanked out the last quill.

I doused my bandana with alcohol and rubbed Gruella's muzzle with it. I gathered my feet underneath me, getting ready to let Gruella up. But first I pushed down on his head to keep him pinned until Howard got out of the way. I nodded to my friend. He slipped the rope loops off Gruella's feet and off his neck. I vaulted off at the same time Howard scuttled backward. Gruella threw his head sideways, rocking onto his belly. Folding his legs underneath him, he pitched to his feet. He shook his body and then wiggled his lips. He lowered his head and softly watched us with deep, brown eyes.

Howard coiled his lariat, patted Gruella, and grumped, "Quit poking your nose where it doesn't belong."

I smiled and stroked the now-docile horse. I turned to thank Howard, but he was already stepping into his pickup. He didn't wait for thanks or acknowledgment. He'd gotten everything he needed from that warm feeling that comes to your heart when you know you've done the right thing. I waved as he pulled away.

Over the years I watched Howard and his wife, Margaret, bless people in the community in the same low-key way. When Howard died a few years back, he left behind a legacy of helping folks on the sly. What I admired Howard and Margaret for the most was taking in a floundering teenage boy and raising him as their own son. They were good people.

Lord, thank You for sending help and an example of how to graciously do things in secret. Amen.

40

Go Left

*Seek his will in all you do, and
he will show you which path to take.*

PROVERBS 3:6 NLT

I stood next to Czar. I was holding the reins and gawking at the sheer rock face of Scapegoat Mountain that glowed gold with the morning sunlight. The short bunch grass rippled in the breeze, and tall spikes of pink fireweed danced. I was in the middle of a summer pack trip. Last night we'd pitched our green tents in Halfmoon Park, a crescent-shaped grassy meadow that hangs shelflike under the Continental Divide. This morning my boss, Bill, was staying behind to help pack mules and pull string. Doug, one of the wranglers, and I would ride ahead with the guests. I was excited about getting started because I'd never ridden this 20-mile stretch. I rubbed Czar's neck and hollered to the guests, "Daylight's burning!"

As the guests gathered their sack lunches and gravitated through the meadow toward their saddle horses, many of their parting words to the wranglers were, "Good luck today." Each time I heard the word "luck" I bristled. *How can you believe in luck?* I wondered. *Do you really believe we're merely victims of happenstance—good or bad?* I kicked the toe of my boot into the dirt.

Saddles groaned as 10 guests, Doug, and I swung up. With Doug in the lead, the horses strung out in a long line that snaked through the grassy meadow and into the pines.

We were well on our way as sunlight streamed through the pine boughs, casting slivers of light across the slope. In front of me the sweaty horses ambled down the narrow trail that clung to the side of the mountain. For miles their hooves clattered along the trail. I turned around. Behind me, high up on the mountain, was the head of Green Fork River. The trail followed along the edge of the narrow gorge all the way to the valley. Directly below the trail the river crashed over boulders, sending a fine mist into the air that glowed in greens, blues, reds, and golds in the refracted light.

A cool breeze drifted up from the river. As the trail wound around a curve in the mountain, I heard the crashing of a waterfall. Czar's ears pricked forward. I watched the cliff on the other side of the river with anticipation. Each of Czar's steps brought us closer. A tan rock rose straight up out of the river, forming a wall that towered several hundred feet. Czar lumbered a few more steps and then I saw it. Across the gap, almost halfway down from the rim, was an enormous cave. A full-sized river spouted out of it and cascaded into a deep pool of roiling water before flowing down the mountain. Arches of rainbows crowned the mist.

Although the trail was no more than a ledge, Doug stopped his horse. The pounding of the water was deafening. The guests stopped behind Doug. Rummaging through their saddlebags, the guys and gals excitedly chattered as they searched for cameras. I gazed in wonder. I'd never seen a river blasting out of the *side* of a mountain like water shooting out of a fire hose. *How many bazillion gallons of water are spewing out of the cave? Where does it come from? Why doesn't the water end?* I rubbed Czar's neck. The cool spray from the waterfall speckled us. Scott, two horses in front of me, pushed back his cowboy hat to snap some pictures.

Doug watched until the last guest tucked his camera away. He picked up the reins and nudged his horse forward. As the horses moved, we all kept our eyes riveted on the waterfall until it was out of sight. Scott glanced back at me. "Rebecca, you're lucky to live here."

I bowed my head and chewed on my lip. I knew he meant no harm, but again I wanted to ask, "Do you really believe in luck? Do you really believe that things just happen with no plan or purpose? What about God? Do you believe in Him?" My heart ached for God. How did He feel when people gave luck credit for things that turned out the way they wanted? I sighed and gathered my reins. Looking at him, I lightly replied, "I'm blessed to live here." How could I begin to explain that I'd been guided here by God? That there wasn't any luck involved?

The next few miles the trail skirted the mountainside above the gorge and the river thundered below. Once again my mind wrestled with the concept of people placing their trust in happenstance. I thought about the time when Amos the mule had been wedged upside down in an avalanche chute. After I prayed for God to send His ministering angels to rescue Amos, he suddenly flipped over and landed on his feet. *I suppose that some people would call that luck,* I groused.

The trail wound through the pines on a flat bench now. Czar slowed as the horses in front of me stopped. I stood in my stirrups, craning my neck to see past the guests' horses to catch sight of Doug. He'd stopped at a fork in the trail. He was digging through his saddlebags and finally pulled out a map. Unfolding it, he glanced at the mountains around him to get his bearings. Saddles creaked as guests turned around, anxiously exchanging glances.

I reined Czar off the trail, nudged him forward, and rode past the guests and up to the front. Doug looked my way as he pushed up his rectangular, wire-rim glasses. I grinned and pointed to the left. He nodded and folded the map. I turned Czar around and rode past the guests to the back of the line. They smiled and looked relieved. Czar fell in behind the last horse.

The August sun warmed us as we wove in and out of tall pines. *Luck.* Rocking in the saddle, my mind turned down memory lane. I remembered when I was alone in hunting camp for four days. It was my job to keep the grizzlies out of camp, and the night before a grizzly had come in and eaten some leftovers. But just that day I'd read an article about the power of praying Psalm 91 for protection. Scared, I'd prayed that psalm each day and asked God to post His angels around camp to keep the bears out. Judging from signs, the grizzlies had circled camp those four days. Not one came in. *I suppose some folks would call that luck too.*

The drum of hoofbeats slowed again. I stretched in my saddle, glancing beyond the guests. Doug had stopped his horse by another fork. The map crinkled as he pulled it out of his saddlebags. The guests fidgeted and then turned to see where I was. Nudging Czar off the trail, I rode past the guests and up to Doug. The map lay open on his lap. Still looking down, he took off his tan cowboy hat and ran his hand through his hair. He kept glancing around at the peaks while he traced his finger along the trail marked on the map. I reined in. "Take a left," I directed. The guests nodded at me as I rode to the back and pulled in behind the last horse.

I gazed around me at the mountains on every side. As we moseyed down the trail into a narrow valley, the horses' hooves began to kick up small clouds of dust. From high branches in the pines, squirrels scolded and chickadees chattered. My mind was still dueling with the word "luck." *How could I possibly attribute all the "coincidences" I've had to luck?* My mind flashed through the memories: the day we got to camp to discover that a grizzly had stormed in and exacted his revenge on us for taking his deer—but we weren't there. The time I lost my watch in the middle of the wilderness…in long grass…but found it 10 days later. The encouraging words I was given that saved a blind colt's life because his eyes and vision just hadn't fully formed yet. The lost mule wearing hobbles caught on some brush that we found in a faraway, tiny meadow. Roman acting as a seeing-eye mule for night-blind Melinda. Hamster teaching a wrangler not to snore so the rest of us could get some sleep. The list was endless. *How could anyone think all these occurrences were due to luck?*

As we moved down the trail that was now mostly rock, once again the line slowed and stopped. The map rattled as Doug opened it. Again I reined Czar off the trail and nudged him forward. The guests watched as I headed forward. When I rode past Scott, he asked, "You know where we are, don't you, Rebecca?"

As Czar plodded forward I looked into Scott's brown eyes and grinned. "Nope. Never been here before."

Scott's face turned a little pale, and the listening guests fidgeted. Doug quizzically looked up at me as I pushed Czar next to his horse and casually pointed on the map to a peak named Triple Divide. I grinned and pointed to the peak on our left. Doug looked at the map and then at the peak. He smiled.

I turned Czar. It was deathly quiet except for Czar's hooves hitting the trail and the sounds of the forest. We moved past the wide-eyed guests who kept looking at me and then at Doug. As I passed Scott I nodded and said, "Don't worry. Bill's behind us, and he can track an ant." Scott pinned a grin on his face and the other guests sat back in their saddles.

Czar pulled in behind the last horse. Doug nudged his horse forward. I rocked comfortably in the saddle when Czar started up again. It seemed strange and at the same time humorous that I'd never ridden this country before but knew which turns to take when the trail forked. We were headed into one of my favorite spots—Danaher Valley. All day long, as we rode down from the Continental Divide, I'd had a bird's-eye view of the wilderness. The peaks that towered around us were the same ones I'd often seen from Danaher...only now I was seeing them from the back side. When I gazed at Triple Divide, a thought clicked into place. I knew where we were because I knew where we were going. And that was much like my life. I'd dedicated my life to Christ. I was headed toward Him. He was the center of my thoughts.

And I saw His presence, power, and protection all around me, providing a map for His trail.

My heart ached for the people who don't know Him. What would life be like if a person didn't know where he or she was going? What would it be like to believe life was just using up time—for no particular reason—until you died? What if a person just drifted into good circumstances and then into bad with no rhyme or reason? I shuddered. *A person would feel lost and alone most of the time.* I glanced at the long line of riders in front of me. *Why am I bristling at their comments instead of praying that their hearts be open to God?*

As the guests took in the splendor around them, I prayed, *God, please touch their hearts in an intimate way while they are here in the wilderness.*

I didn't hear any specifics about how God touched them...or if they felt His touch, but I'm sure He responded to my prayer. And He certainly flooded my heart with the gift of compassion.

> *Lord, fill my heart with compassion and remind me to pray for the people around me, especially when they credit luck for their good fortune. Amen.*

41

Dastardly Guest

If you love those who love you, what credit is that to you?
Even "sinners" love those who love them.

LUKE 6:32

The August sun blistered the soil. The air was still except for the droning of the annoying horseflies. Darrin sat on a camp chair under the green kitchen tarp drinking Kool-Aid. Pork chops sizzled on the cast-iron grill on the stove. I stirred green beans. It had been a long, sweltering ride today, just like it had been the previous three days. I sipped some Kool-Aid and nudged Darrin. "Did you see what Hal did?"

Darrin shook his head and leaned forward. I whispered, "Look at this place. It looks like God rained rocks down from heaven into this little bowl. So when we rode into camp I quickly tied up Czar and scouted out a good tent site for the older guests Nancy and Ruth. I figured their bones would appreciate a spot without rocks."

Darrin nodded in agreement.

I slid the kettle of beans to a cooler spot on the stove and lowered my voice even more. "As soon as I turned back to get Nancy and

Ruth, Hal walked up, threw his gear down on the spot I'd chosen, and announced in his monotone voice that it was *his* campsite. And since he was a guest, I couldn't really say anything."

A fly landed on my jeans. I swatted it and glanced across the camp at the rope corral. Hal untied his slicker from his saddle and carried it to his tent. I frowned as I looked at his young, tall, strong body. *How can anybody be so selfish?* I wondered. I glanced across the meadow and watched Nancy tuck a gray strand of hair under her cowboy hat while she unzipped the door flap on their green tent. Ruth slowly hobbled over, carrying their sleeping bags. Glancing at Darrin, I growled, "Of all the gall. To steal a campsite from two older ladies!"

Darrin whispered, "Have you watched him ride his horse?"

I nodded and mimicked Hal slouching in the saddle and staring at the saddle horn. We both chuckled.

I reached for the pitcher and poured another glass of Kool-Aid. "What does his girlfriend see in him anyway? He acts like a robot. I haven't seen him show any enthusiasm or interest yet. It's a good thing he's a computer whiz because he sure doesn't have any communication skills—not even with his horse. Maybe we should mount a keyboard on his saddle horn."

Darrin and I both laughed again. Using tongs I took the pork chops off the griddle and put them in a large kettle so I could dish them out one by one. Just thinking about having to pass out the meat this way made me boil. Normally I'd place the platter of meat on the serving table where the guests dished up buffet style. But on the first night of the trip, Hal had taken *seven* pieces of chicken the first time through the line. *Couldn't he see that there were 14 more people standing in line behind him?* I'd thought disgustedly. I'd packed loads of a variety of foods, but I didn't think someone would be so rude as to eat most of the meat himself, especially since he hadn't listed any special "dietary needs" on his registration form. The platter of chicken had been empty by the time the wranglers and I got to the buffet table. We went without.

I cupped my hand next to my mouth and yelled, "Dinner!" The guests meandered their way through the rocks...except Hal. He charged his way to the front of the line. Towering over everyone, he grabbed a plate and piled it high. I looked at Darrin and rolled my eyes. *I can't wait until we take this guy back to the ranch and watch him drive away. Six more days—and counting.*

The next few days Hal made everyone miserable. His pushy "me me me" attitude created tension between everyone. Maybe it wouldn't have been so bad if he would've smiled, or laughed, or talked to the other guests. But he never showed any emotion at all. Nor did he seem interested in anybody or anything...except his girlfriend.

By the seventh day I disliked him so much I didn't bother talking to him. That morning a brisk breeze blew as we rode the horses up the side of a mountain and into the high country. Cotton-ball clouds lazily drifted across the deep-blue sky. The long line of riders snaked across the windswept mountainside. Riding above the tree line, we could see rows of snowcapped peaks stretching like a ribbon all the way to Canada. As the horses walked along the rocky trail, every guest gawked at the big sky Montana was known for. Well, everyone except Hal, who slouched in his saddle, stared at the saddle horn, and kept the reins looped so long they slapped his horse's neck with every step.

As the wind began to howl across the top of the trees, we rounded a corner and rode into a rock-lined bowl. A seep of water ran through the little meadow, filling it with lush grass. We reined in and stopped for lunch.

After dismounting, we slipped off the bridles, leaving the halters on. We hung the bridles on the saddle horns and led them by the lead ropes to a cluster of boulders surrounded by grass. The animals instantly dropped their heads to graze. Because we were above the tree line, there wasn't anyplace to tie the horses, so some of us loosely held on to the lead ropes. The animals that could be trusted not to wander were allowed to roam the small meadow, their lead ropes hooked to the saddles.

We pulled our lunches out of the saddle bags and sat down on the rocks. I settled in and took a bite of my peanut butter sandwich. My favorite bright-pink flower caught my eye as it swayed in the breeze. "Oh, you guys have got to see this!" I bounded off the boulder and ran to the clump of flowers. Gently I picked the six-inch stalk and trotted back to the guests. All eyes were on me...except Hal's. I passed the flower to Nancy. Gingerly she took it.

I bent over her shoulder. "See all these one-inch flowers that line the stalk both vertically and horizontally? Look closely at one of them."

Nancy pushed back her hat and gazed at it.

I pointed. "There must be at least 25 individual flowers on that stalk, and each one looks like a miniature elephant head. See the two big-floppy ears on either side of the faces and the hook-shaped trunks? That's why it's called an elephant-head flower."

Nancy gawked. "I've never seen anything so exquisite!" She passed the flower to Ruth.

Ruth exclaimed, "How magnificent!"

Hal was sitting next to Ruth. He hadn't been interested in anything on the trip, so Ruth naturally reached around him to pass the flower to his girlfriend. But Hal reached out his large hand. Ever so gently he cradled the blooms. His eyes grew wide as he gently rolled the stem in his fingers and the elephant heads twirled. A smile cracked across his face. His eyes glistened as he exclaimed, "This is beautiful!"

Shocked, I looked at him. *There's a person who lives inside that body.* I was amazed.

Delightedly he touched an elephant trunk with his finger. "Do they grow other places too?"

I shrugged. "I've only found them in the high country...and close to water. I don't know if they grow in other states."

Tenderly Hal caressed a floppy ear. Minutes passed as the guests watched Hal come to life. Finally he passed the flower to his girlfriend.

I continued to look at him. A horrible feeling gnawed in my spirit.

There is a person in there. A person who has feelings. A person God created. And I've been treating him like he's a robot. Sure he is selfish and rude, but did I have the right to make fun of him? He had been unlovable, but I had been unlovable in return.

For the next few days I picked flowers to show the guests. Hal was interested in some, but not in others. He still shoved to be the first in the chow line and always chose the best campsites for himself. But something had changed inside me. I now looked at him as one of God's creations.

After the trip was over, I stood on the porch at the ranch and waved goodbye. In a way, I was sad to see him go. Maybe if he'd stayed another week, he would have crawled a bit further out of his shell. I'd learned an incredibly valuable lesson from him. No matter how a person acts, I need to treat him or her as though God created the person special—because He did.

> *Lord, there are times when I'm unlovable yet You continue to love me. Thank You for that! Remind me to do the same for others. Amen.*

42

Cowboy Hat Rodeo

Let us, therefore, make every effort to enter that
rest, so that no one will fall.

HEBREWS 4:11

Thirteen saddled horses dozed as they stood next to the pines they were tied to. Each horse had a hind leg cocked in relaxation and a bottom lip that drooped. The light morning breeze rustled through the knee-deep, tan grass of the Danaher Valley. Britt, my palomino gelding, gently nudged me. I stood by his side, reins in hand, waiting. Of the ten guests, only two had stuffed their lunch sacks into their saddlebags and tied their slickers on the back of their saddles. A few stood around the fire pit chatting, even though we'd doused the flames an hour ago. The rest watched the wranglers pack the loads on the mules. I glanced at them and muttered, "Hurry up! Didn't you hear Bill holler 'Daylight's burning' over five minutes ago? Hello, people! That means get on your horses because we're leaving."

I'd been in a rush since I crawled out of my sleeping bag this morning. It was the first week of August. The crew had worked together all summer, and we'd perfected the way we pulled together as a team.

183

From the moment we opened our eyes, we moved with speed and skill as we caught and saddled the stock, cooked breakfast, tore down camp, and packed the mules. We didn't waste a minute. Our goal was to get the guests out of camp as soon as possible so they could enjoy the day on the trail. The wranglers would stay behind packing the mules. While the guests stopped to eat lunch, the wranglers would pass them and ride ahead to set up camp.

Bill stood by his horse's side, slapping his reins against his leg. He shouted, "Let's mount up." His voice echoed through the brisk air and down the meadow.

A horsefly droned past and settled on Britt. He switched his tail and stomped his foot. I brushed it off and watched the guests wander toward their horses. *Put some hustle in your bustle. We're wasting time!* I wanted to chant "Go…go…go!" It was going to be an exceptionally long ride up Limestone Pass today. I wanted to jump in the saddle *now* so we wouldn't be riding in the dark.

The riders nonchalantly tied their slickers behind their saddles and bridled their horses. Britt impatiently stomped his foot. I stroked his cheek. "I know. But getting them moving is like pushing a wet noodle." I twirled the end of the lead rope.

Finally saddles creaked as a couple of them stepped up. I checked Britt's cinch, gathered the reins, and swung into the saddle. But before I finished settling in, one of the guests crawled out of his saddle saying, "Oh, I left my lunch by the fire pit." I rolled my eyes as several others climbed down to retrieve their bags.

I wiggled in my saddle, not wanting to sit still. I reached down and patted my horse's golden neck. "Well, Britt, it's your lucky day. No sense in wasting time just sitting here." At best, Britt was green broke. Going down the trail he listened most of the time, but there were still some things that would pull his trigger, like if I put on my slicker while still in the saddle. Even though I'd sacked him out a bazillion times—meaning I'd flapped and moved saddle pads, slickers, canvas pieces, and cowboy hats around him so he'd get used to noise and movement—sometimes he'd still snort and blow and then launch toward the moon. I needed to work with him more. *Why not now?* I nodded. *But I don't want to start with the slicker.* I looked at the jackets tied to my saddle. *What's smaller?* I smiled and grasped the brim of my black cowboy hat.

Britt's eyes followed the hat as I lifted it off my head and set it on my right knee. I counted to 10 then put it back on my head. He was alert, but calm. Reaching down, I stroked his neck. "Good boy." I did that a few more times, setting it on my right knee. He swiveled his ears and watched closely. I switched to setting it on my left knee. After the fourth time, he breathed a deep sigh and relaxed. I slipped my hat on my head and glanced around at the guests, who were now chatting with the wranglers. Gritting my teeth I murmured, "What's holding us up now?"

I pulled off my hat and rubbed it over the top of Britt's withers. I put it back on my head. No reaction. Next I rubbed both sides of his neck with my hat. He calmly stood as if this were normal. I lifted the hat and put it toward his head. He turned his nose around to sniff it. My saddle groaned as I leaned off the right side, stretching so he could get a good whiff. Suddenly he snorted and jumped back. I fell forward in the saddle. Grabbing on with my left hand I quickly pulled to center my balance—only that movement jerked my right hand with the hat toward Britt's face. He thought the hat was chasing him. He blew hard and jumped sideways. With my right hand, I grabbed to hang on, making the hat lunge for him again. With a loud snort, he orbited toward the clouds and came down stiff-legged. Being off balance from the start, I now dangled off the right side. He shot into the sky and started bucking mid-air. I hung on for all I was worth. He hammered the ground again and again. Each time I lost a couple inches.

A fury of power surged through him. He exploded into a cyclone. The world spun around as I grabbed hold. He dropped his head and threw himself forward...and then back...and then he leaped into the air.

Slamming the earth with his front feet, he kicked out both hind legs. Dirt flew from beneath his feet. He spun in tight circles. A cloud of dust boiled around us.

He leaped in the air again, twisting his body and flinging me off like I was a ragdoll. Airborne, I somersaulted backward. Whop! Both his hind feet nailed me in the center of my back as I was falling. Pain shot through me. Wham! I slammed into some rocks, knocking the breath out of me.

Stars floated through a black haze. I blinked and looked up. All the guests were leaning over me. "Are you okay?" one of them asked.

Humiliated, I wanted to crawl under a rock. A wave of nauseousness washed over me. I wiggled my toes and moved my legs, checking to make sure everything was okay. As I moved my arm I gasped. A bolt of pain seared through my ribs. I lay still, only wanting to rest.

Rebecca, if you would have rested ten minutes ago, you wouldn't be in this fix. I listened to God continue. *Why did you push, push, push?*

Bill squatted next to me, concern lining his face. "Are you okay?"

I grunted and then said, "I think I broke some ribs. Other than that, I think so."

Bill scratched the back of his head. "Are you able to ride?"

I nodded. "I might need help getting on Britt though."

Slowly I stood, careful not to jar my ribs. While I brushed myself off, the guests mounted up. Bill led Britt into a small dip next to me. Hobbling over, I picked up my hat, shook out the dirt, wiped it clean, and pulled it down tight on my head.

Britt's eyes were rimmed in white when I walked up to him. "I'm sorry, buddy." I gently reached for his neck and stroked him. After a few minutes he sighed and relaxed. I gasped with pain as I pulled myself into the saddle.

The remainder of the day was torturous as we climbed the rocky trail leading to Limestone Pass. Every jolt wiggled those ribs and sent waves of pain through me. Over those 18 miles I cross-examined myself, trying to get to why I'd refused to stop and take a break. My go-go-go attitude wasn't just about getting down the trail before dark. It was deeper than that. I'd been irritated with the guests. Instead of patiently explaining to them that we had a long day, I'd stuffed that fact inside, expecting them to read my mind. Before long my impatience had boiled over and riled up my spirit.

Why hadn't I explained and then patiently waited...or even helped them? My lack of communication leading to frustration and irritation had been *my* choice. It had nothing to do with the guests' actions.

For the rest of the trip the guests and crew pitched in to help me cook and serve meals. I gratefully rested every chance possible, especially while waiting for the guests to get going in the mornings. Britt never did get over his spookiness even though I tried to work him through it. Every time I rode him, I was reminded to "live in God's rest."

Lord, thank You for reminding me that I choose my responses to situations. At any time I can choose to walk in Your tracks and be patient, kind, and live in Your rest. Amen.

43

Coleman Lantern

*In the same way, let your light shine before men, that they may see
your good deeds and praise your Father in heaven.*

MATTHEW 5:16

The first glimmers of dawn glowed in the sky. The October breeze
rustled my wickiup, a low slung tarp I used instead of a tent. Curled
in the bottom of the red mummy sleeping bag, I lay on the ground. Last
night it was so cold that I'd pulled the drawstring on the hood tight,
leaving only a small opening. Rye, my German shepherd, stretched and
yawned. She romped through the meadow. Thundering back, she
stuck her cold, wet nose into my bag and licked my nose. "Come and
play!" I buried my head deeper in the bag. "Yuck! Stop it, Rye! What's
so great about this morning? It's cold out there!"

Rye leaned her body against the sleeping bag and plopped to the
ground, resting her head on her paws right in front of me, waiting to
lick my face again as soon as it showed.

I sat up to avoid her licks and pulled open the drawstring. I blinked.
"Snow!"

The wickiup sagged under the weight. The small meadow was

covered with at least four inches of white stuff. "Ugh." I flopped on my side, burying my face inside the sleeping bag.

It was my first season working as a wilderness ranger for the Forest Service. I'd outfitted in the Bob Marshall Wilderness Complex for years, but I'd always worked in crews and had guests along. This year was different. All summer and fall I'd worked alone, riding Czar and packing my gear on Little Girl, my brown mule. In the summer I'd collected wilderness data, and this fall I was inspecting hunting camps. At first it was great. I loved the freedom of not being concerned about guests. I explored new trails and enjoyed my small, simple camps that consisted of a wickiup and a one-burner propane stove. But after being alone all summer and fall, I was missing the camaraderie of people. Loneliness crept into my soul. I sighed. *All I'm going to see today are strangers, if that.* Most of the time the camps were empty because the people were out hunting. I was 17 miles into the wilderness area, and there was only a slim chance I'd see someone I knew. *It sure would be nice to see a familiar face and sit around a campfire listening to stories.* The snow slid off my wickiup. I braced myself for the cold and climbed out of the sleeping bag.

After munching a bowl of granola and sipping a steaming cup of coffee, I broke camp and stepped into the saddle. I rode toward the first hunting camp on my list. When I arrived, not a soul was around. I checked the camp over. Everything was in order, so I mounted up and rode on. By the time I sat on a boulder next to a rumbling creek to eat crackers and tuna for lunch, I hadn't even seen a stranger.

The sun glistened off the snow, melting it. Piles fell from pine boughs as chickadees chattered. I slipped into the saddle. Czar and Little Girl slogged down the muddy trail toward Cooney Creek Camp. In previous years I'd worked for the outfitter who ran that camp. I'd heard he had a new crew this year. When I rode into the grassy meadow, I was shocked to hear a woman's voice call, "Hey, Rebecca! Is that you?"

I nudged Czar closer. Cocking my head to the side, I eyed the brown-haired, small woman walking toward me. Rye ran full-blast to her, wiggling around her legs while the woman petted her.

Then I recognized her. She'd been a guest on a couple of my pack trips. "Jacque?" I asked. "What are you doing here?"

Tipping her head to the side, Jacque grinned. "Jack needed a cook for this hunt, and I was able to take a vacation from my job."

I slipped out of the saddle, and we gave each other a hug. Huddling next to the wood cookstove, we sipped coffee and caught up on each other's lives. I glanced at my watch. "I still have to check this camp and a couple more. I'd better get going."

Jacque nodded but added, "Why don't you come back for dinner? Will seven o'clock tonight work?"

I grinned. "You bet!"

The rest of the afternoon whirled past. With a light heart I checked camps. When I reined Czar toward Cooney Creek, it was so dark outside I couldn't see my hand in front of my face. The sun had set over an hour ago. The air was still, broken only by an occasional owl hooting, Rye's snuffling along the trail, and Czar and Little Girl's hooves trudging through the mud. The stars appeared one by one, twinkling in the cobalt-blue sky. With each of Czar's steps I moved rhythmically in the saddle, watching the whitish band of the Milky Way appear. A half-hour passed. Czar rounded the foot of the mountain. In the distance a Coleman lantern glowed from the corral at Cooney Creek Camp. Its light was so warm and inviting. *How fitting.* Ever since Jacque had invited me for dinner, I hadn't felt lonely—even riding through the empty wilderness in the dark of the night. Her small act of kindness lit up my day and life.

After taking care of Czar, I huddled with the guests around the long, plank kitchen table near the woodstove. I relished the roast beef dinner complete with mashed potatoes and gravy. Pushing back from the table, we shared stories and laughter filled that white canvas tent until the wee hours. Finally it was time to go so everyone could get some rest before our next day's work and hunt.

I said my goodbyes and got Czar ready. My saddle creaked as I turned Czar away from the lantern. *God, only You could have set this up. You knew I'd be lonely today. Thank You for sending Jacque to be one of the "new" crew in Cooney Creek.* Riding into the black night the short distance to where I planned to camp, my heart glowed from Jacque's kindness…and God's thoughtfulness.

Lord, thank You for putting people in my life who reflect Your love. Show me opportunities where I can shine Your light on the people around me through random acts of kindness. Amen.

44

Raining Ashes

*I remind you to fan into flame the
gift of God, which is in you.*

2 Timothy 1:6

With my red bandana I wiped away the sweat that dripped down my neck. The sun felt unusually hot. My throat was raw from breathing the dry air because humidity levels were at all-time lows. I rode Britt, my dark palomino gelding. The drumbeat of 40 hoofs sounded behind me as 10 guests and their horses drifted along. The trail wound through lodgepole pines and then down switchbacks to the base of the mountain and Burnt Cabin. Relaxed, I rocked side to side in sync with Britt's stride as I mulled over a Bible verse I'd read that morning. It talked about fanning into flame the gift of God inside me. *God, I don't understand. How do I do that? How does that apply to me?* I lived in the woods from May through December, so it wasn't like I could go to church or join a Bible study to get more information.

Britt hesitated at a fork in the trail. I touched the reins gently on his neck, guiding him toward the Monture trailhead. As soon as he realized he was headed home, he stretched his legs at a faster clip. I swayed back in the saddle and drew him in a bit. "I know, only nine more miles to go." Today was the last day of a weeklong summer trip. Britt splashed into Burnt Cabin Creek as it gurgled over pebbles. Thirsty, he lowered his head and sucked water. I leaned back in the saddle and frowned. A plume of smoke was rising from the backside of the mountain on my left.

A forest fire caused by lightning had started at the beginning of the summer. The Forest Service had decided to let it burn. In June and July its flaming fingers smoldered through the valleys and over the mountains. The fire moved in fits and spurts. Sometimes the flames only licked a couple acres; other times it scorched hundreds.

Working in conjunction with the Forest Service, we rerouted our summer trips to skirt the flames. Oftentimes the smoke would lazily drift through our campsites at night, dropping cold ashes on us. During the day it wasn't uncommon to ride through thick smoke to get to our next camp. We viewed the fire as an inconvenient, but natural, occurrence in the wilderness area.

At the beginning of August, the temperatures had soared, drying out the forest. Now flames erupted in thousands of acres. Gray plumes roiled and rose hundreds of feet into the sky before mushrooming like an atomic bomb cloud. Many evenings when we camped in the high country, the guests and crew would sit on a nearby ridge at sunset. With fascination we watched the meandering flames in the valleys below.

Shaking my head, I came back to the present. Britt picked up his head, and water gushed out the sides of his mouth. I nudged him forward slowly. The guests' horses clattered over the rocks as they spread out in the creek before pausing to drink. After the last horse lifted its head, I tapped Britt's sides and he started a fast walk through the pine flats. Soon the trail narrowed along a grassy hillside. We rounded a bend. In shock I blinked and halted Britt. Blood drained out of my face as I felt the ball of heat that was rolling over the mountain. Ash was raining down. Only this time it included small, red-glowing embers. *How can this be?* I wondered. Squinting, I scanned the eastern horizon.

I could see where the plume was, indicating the active fire—and it was more than seven miles away.

A hot breeze boiled around us. An ember fell on Britt. Quickly I flicked it off. My mind whirled. A fire needs three things: heat, oxygen, and fuel. This heat moving before the main fire was drying out the forest, prepping it to really burn fast and hot. *If we get any kind of wind, the forest around us is going to explode.* I knew that it would probably take days or even weeks for that to happen, but I still tipped back the brim of my hat and glanced to the west, where our prevailing storms originated. *Clear sky. We won't get any wind before we get to the trailhead.*

My saddle creaked as I turned around and hollered to the white-eyed guests, "Let's boogey out of here." All the guests gathered their reins and kicked their horses into a fast walk. Mile after mile we gawked at the boiling white plume. Finally a cool breeze enveloped us, and only an occasional ember floated past. We made it through the potentially dangerous spot without anybody—human or animal—getting burned.

It was then that a "still, small voice" spoke to my spirit: "My Word is like the embers. Your will is like the oxygen. And your deeds are the fuel. When you study My Word and set your will in agreement, it prepares your heart. Out of your heart, your deeds will produce My holy fire."

The final ember of the trip fell on my shoulder. I brushed it off and grinned. *Lord, I'm going to pack myself so full of Your Word I will explode with Your fire!*

> *God, give me an unquenchable thirst for Your Word. I love You. Amen.*

45

Firestorm!

When Lot lived, people were also eating and drinking.
They were buying, selling, planting, and building.
But on the very day Lot left Sodom, fiery flames
poured down from the sky and killed everyone.

LUKE 17:28-29 CEV

I strolled through the tall grass out on the point overlooking the Danaher Valley to view the sunset—and watch the columns of smoke from the forest fire that was southeast of us and about eight miles away. Horses and mules munched grass in the little meadow behind me. Sitting down, I tucked my legs to the side and leaned on my arm. Across the valley a coyote howled. An unusually hot evening wind swirled through. It was the end of the first week in September. I'd been setting up a hunting camp with four crew members. Eight days from now we'd be packing in our first guests. We'd already set up the white canvas wall tents with cots inside, tacked a green tarp over a log frame for the hay shed, and unpacked and arranged the kitchen tent. Today we finished here, so tomorrow we'd be packing our gear and riding the 18 miles to Cooney Creek to set up a second hunting camp.

A wind gust from the east grabbed for my cowboy hat. I pulled it down tight as I searched the horizon. These days it was my nightly routine to watch the black and billowing plumes of smoke from the fire. It had started back in June. The Forest Service had deemed it a "prescribed burn within the wilderness," so it was allowed to burn without human intervention. At first it had grown slowly, burning a narrow finger of forest. The fire and embers smoldered and slithered, creating a mosaic of green trees and blackened land.

As the summer temperatures rose, the fire grew in intensity. Some days it would blow up and consume hundreds of acres. Then it would die down and inch along for a while. We'd been dodging it all summer on our pack trips and were tired of breathing its smoke and smelling its odor. Living with it day-in and day-out lulled us into accepting the stinky thing. It was an inconvenience we tolerated. The only interesting thing was watching the black smoke rise high into the sky. At night the plumes glowed.

Another wind gust picked up small pebbles and threw them at me. Pine needles hurled past. Fascinated, I stared as the smoke boiled and roiled. The wind swayed the columns of black smoke to-and-fro. Suddenly the fire exploded into one large flame that mushroomed as if someone had poured gasoline on it. I held my breath. *Those flames must be 300 feet tall!* The flames swept up, seeming to engulf the entire mountainside at once. Sweeping through the pines, the inferno crowned the top of the mountain. Trees exploded, spraying flares of red and gold. The fire belched black soot.

Wide-eyed, I watched the fire rage. From behind another mountain, several fires rolled around the front, leaving streaks of flaming trees in their wakes. The wind grabbed them and swept them together into another wall of flame. For hours I watched as the "harmless inconvenience" turned into a raging dynamo—a fast-moving, wind-driven firestorm. With a whoosh it devoured whole gullies. Later I learned the flames had gusted at more than 50 miles per hour and had formed a 50-mile wall.

As night settled, I continued to watch the orange and red flames lick the horizon as far as I could see. I rubbed my eyes. *It must be at least one o'clock. I need to get some sleep.* In the dark I strolled toward my tent, sifting my thoughts. I hadn't believed the fire would amount to anything. After all, we'd lived with it for months. *And now it seemed to blow up so suddenly.* A mosquito bit me. I slapped it. *Suddenly? It wasn't a sudden thing. It was building an arsenal all summer.*

I cast a parting glance over my shoulder just as a tree exploded with a loud crackle, sending flames shooting up like fireworks. *Was this what it was like in the times of Sodom and Gomorrah? The people had been lulled into thinking there wasn't anything wrong with their lifestyles. They ignored all the warning signs and partied the days away—until fire rained from the sky.* I inhaled deeply. There were areas in my life where the devil had been playing a country-western tune...and I was tapping my toes to it. I sighed. *If I listen to that tune long enough, the next thing I know I'll be dancing with the devil. It's time to stop the music and listen to God's voice.*

> *Lord, I don't want to be caught off guard when You come back. Open my eyes to the things I need to change...and give me the courage to follow through. Amen.*

46

Drifts of Ashes

The faithful love of the LORD never ends! His mercies never cease.
Great is his faithfulness; his mercies begin afresh each morning.

LAMENTATIONS 3:22-23 NLT

The putrid smell of the fire hung ominously in the blistery hot morning breeze that rattled through the pine needles. The trail wound through the valley bottom before moving across the foot of the nearby mountain. Jack rode his mule in front of me. Behind me were three guys on crew, each leading a string of mules. The hard-packed dirt trail was so dry that miniature clouds of dust boiled up and swirled around us with each step the horses and mules took. From the top of our cowboy hats to the bottom of our boots, we were coated with tan grit. Worse than that was the grit that smothered our souls. We rocked in our saddles and wondered, *Will anything be left after this forest fire?* The air was so dry I had a sore throat and my mouth was sticky. I reached around and unbuckled my saddlebags. Pulling out my water bottle, I took a swig. Almost instantly my mouth was dry again.

Yesterday we'd finished setting up at Danaher, and today we were riding to Cooney Creek to set up camp. We were expecting the hunters within a week, but last night may have changed everything. The forest fire that had smoldered and burned all summer had morphed into a full-fledged firestorm. Last night after dark we watched as miles away the wind gusted and merged individual fires into a 50-mile-long wall. It thundered and roared through the wilderness. Gullies and valleys were incinerated within minutes. Flames burst into the sky, crowning the trees on top of several mountains.

Thankfully, early this morning the winds had quit. The fire spigot was shut off, and once again this side of the wilderness was merely smoldering. Tipping up the bottle again, I slowly swished water around my mouth before swallowing. *I'd better save some, it's going to be a long, dry day,* I reminded myself. I tucked the container in a saddlebag. Glancing at the horizon, there seemed to be smoke from individual fires everywhere. Because we didn't have communication with civilization available, we didn't know what was happening with the fire. We did know we felt surrounded by flames, and last night it looked like the area near the ranch may have burned. No matter which direction we chose to ride out, we would have to dodge around a fire...or ride through one.

The Danaher Valley where we were was still green, but it brimmed with dry grass and pine trees—tons of fuel for the approaching menace. We figured it was safer to be in the black areas where the fire had already consumed everything burnable. Usually around this time of year we would get cooler weather, and the first snows in the high county should arrive soon. That would settle the fire down. We hoped the fire would remain in the distance...and that our paying guests weren't discouraged or considering backing out. Not working this part of the season would hit our pocketbooks pretty hard.

We didn't know if the fire had consumed Cooney Creek Camp, but we would soon find out. Riding around a bend, I reached down and patted Britt's palomino neck. Dust puffed up. *Yuck!* I brushed my hand off on my jeans, and then looked up aghast. A line had been drawn on the mountain. Everything on one side was green; the other side was torched. Tall, charred spires of what used to be pine trees stuck out of gray mounds of ash. Some of the charred stumps lay in piles like pickup sticks, flames still licking at them. The powdery gray ash was cool now and more than a foot deep as far as we could see. Everything was eerily quiet. Not a bird chirped, or a squirrel chattered, or even the drone of a horsefly was heard. They'd been driven out or killed.

The horses shuffled through the ash that muffled the sounds of their hooves. It was like creeping through a graveyard. I turned around, and the saddle noise seemed loud and out of place. Looking at Bill, I whispered, "This looks like pictures I've seen of the moon." Bill frowned and surveyed the devastation.

The trail was covered under the deep ash, so by memory we picked our way across the moonscape, dodging the places where fires still crackled. When we came to North Fork Cabin, Jack reined in his mule. I rode up alongside him. He took off his cowboy hat, ran his hand through his white hair, and looked toward his ranch that was about 12 miles away as the crow flies. With a grim voice he said, "I'm going to head home to see if there's anything left."

I nodded and looked at the smoldering hillsides. The fire had run through the canyon due south—straight toward his place.

Jack took a deep breath and straightened in the saddle. With determination he looked me in the eye. "If it's gone, I'll build it again." He waved to the guys. "See you in a few days."

Somberly we watched him ride away. In those few hours last night, while the inferno raged, Jack may have lost almost everything he possessed. He didn't even know if his wife was okay. But instead of whining, moaning, being a victim, or freaking out, he calmly reached inside himself and made a decision—that no matter what, he would turn this into an opportunity to persevere.

The guys and I turned our horses up Hobnail Tom Trail. We rode between charred spikes of pines interspersed with green patches of forest. We hoped the fire had skipped over camp, but when the horses splashed through Cooney Creek our hopes were dashed. We reined in the horses. The fire had swept through the small meadow nestled between two mountains and incinerated nearly everything. Spot fires still crackled and popped. Wooden corral rails nailed to trees had burned along with everything else. The only things left were short-burning stubs hanging by nails. In some spots the fire had dug into the duff, the thick layer of pine needles, leaves, and debris that formed the forest floor. As this material burned, craters were formed. I shook my head and glanced at Bill. Deep in thought, he wiped his dark moustache. He set his jaw and said, "Let's get unloaded and put these fires out. We've got some long days ahead of us."

I looked for a tree that wasn't on fire so I could tie Britt up. I stepped out of the saddle. I was bursting with admiration for Bill and Jack. There aren't many people in the world who can see opportunity in the face of destruction. And here I was, blessed to work with two of them.

Lord, when I'm hit with destruction in my life, remind me to reach inside and gather strength from You. Help me look at it as an opportunity to start afresh. Amen.

47

Worthless

We are God's masterpiece. He has created us anew in Christ Jesus,
so we can do the good things he planned for us long ago.

EPHESIANS 2:10 NLT

S weat trickled down my back as I sat on the ground in a deep drift
of ashes—almost the only thing the forest fire had left behind. My
sooty hand held a bent nail on a rock as I tapped it with a hammer to
straighten it. It was tedious work. It wouldn't have been so bad if I'd
had an anvil or something flat to lay the nail on. Wiping my forehead,
I longed to sit in the shade, but all the trees at Cooney Creek Camp
had been burned up.

Yesterday our crew—three guys and me—had ridden in and discovered the devastation. Although the meadow had been cremated, a
lot of spots that were good for hunting were unscathed and green, providing habitat for any animals that had hopefully taken refuge there.
In six days we were supposed to be guiding hunters in this area. We'd
been working night and day to rebuild the camp. When getting ready
for the trip, we'd packed as usual because the fire had been smoldering slowly all summer. We never dreamed it would reach this far and

wipe out the camp. The one thing we needed most was a bucket of nails for rebuilding the tent frames and corrals. But we'd only packed enough for minor jobs, and obviously going to the hardware store 17 horseback miles and a 45-minute pickup drive away was out of the question. We were "making do." I'd volunteered to sift through the ashes to find nails to straighten and reuse.

I dug next to the trees that corral rails had been nailed to. When I found nails, I tapped them straight. When a small pile accumulated, I doled them out to the guys, who were nailing in place the new rails they'd cut. For hours I rolled bent and sooty nails across my chosen, semiflat rock, tap, tap, tapping until they were fairly straight. My mind wandered as I grabbed another nail. Bent at a 90-degree angle, it was worthless as it was.

I've felt worthless before. My mind traveled back to when I was a gangly kid with Coke-bottle glasses—glasses so thick they were like the bottom of a Coke bottle. The other kids had nicknamed me "Ocky," short for octopus because my legs and arms were so long. In sports I had a terrible time getting them to go in the right direction at the same time. My mind fast-forwarded to the years I'd spent in different colleges. I'd never fit in and had no clue what to do with my life. I kept dropping out. The worst part was that I started to believe I was worthless. I was headed nowhere fast. Then I started working from the saddle in Montana. I finally fit in! I loved riding a horse all day, and my relationship with God flourished as I faced the challenges and dangers of outdoor life.

Twisting the nail, I tapped it with the hammer. With each danger, it was like God was tap, tap, tapping my life, making my faith strong so my life would be strong, straight, and useable for His purposes. Sometimes it had been uncomfortable, but I was a better person for it. Each time I triumphed, I felt better about me. I pushed the nail across the rock. It rolled flat. "Looks good to me. You're ready to be used...and so am I."

Thank You, Lord, for sifting through the ashes of my life, scooping me up, and tapping me into a person of value to You. Amen.

48

Crying in the Night

As the deer pants for streams of water,
so my soul pants for you, O God.

PSALM 42:1

The sun slipped down, plunging the valley into darkness...except for the red glow of the forest fire that licked up the sides of some of the mountains. Sitting on a charred log, I poked my small campfire with a stick. The fire crackled and popped. The three crewmen I was working with sat on blackened logs next to me. Firelight flickered across our sooty faces. Today we'd worked hard to rebuild Cooney Creek Camp after it was destroyed by the forest fire. Everything we touched had black char on it. When we picked up a log to toss it out of the way, we'd get the charcoal on our hands and clothes. Later, when we'd wipe off sweat, the charcoal would get on our faces...and everywhere else we touched. It wasn't long before we were black from head to toe.

An evening breeze stirred the ash on the ground. The smoke from the campfire shifted, and my eyes watered as I waved it out of my face. I slid to the other end of the log. Bill sat with his arms resting on his knees. He'd cut new corral posts and nailed them to trees all day—grueling work. He leaned forward, picked up a chunk of wood, and set it on the fire. Flames danced. "Tomorrow we'll finish building the corral," he noted. He paused and squinted his eyes at a mountain. He cocked his head.

I listened...and then I heard it: a faint and pitiful cry.

Bill's dark eyebrows creased and compassion flooded his eyes. He looked at his boots and lowered his voice. "It's a fawn crying for its mom. They must have gotten separated when the firestorm raged through here. I hope its mom didn't burn up." He looked up and froze, staring at the next mountain over.

We looked over just in time to watch the wind whip life into the smoldering embers. Flames shot up trees again, making them into torches. A tree exploded, shooting red sparks into the sky. My body felt numb as I watched the wind sweep the flames into an insatiable beast that devoured everything in its path. The flames lit up the black sky...and then gradually died down as the fire front slithered to the other side of the mountain. The faint cry echoed through the forest again. The sound had moved, so the fawn must be wandering around. I tucked a strand of blond hair behind my ear. "I suppose that fawn will cry until it finds its mom or until a coyote or mountain lion finds it." The next hour we watched several mountainsides be engulfed by flames and listened to the fawn's cry. My heart ached but there wasn't anything I could do.

When I crawled into my sleeping bag, that young critter was still out there alone. Nothing was going to satisfy it other than being by its mom's side. I rolled on my side, tucking the sleeping bag around my head to muffle the mournful noise. A worship tune drifted through my memory: "As the deer panteth for the water, so my soul longeth for Thee." *Lord, that is how I want my relationship to be with You. I only want to be satisfied when I'm by Your side.*

Lord, place in my heart a passion for You that will grow deeper each day. Amen.

49

North, South, East, or West?

*Greater love has no one than this, that he lay
down his life for his friends.*

JOHN 15:13

G ray Camp Robbers flew in and squawked and begged for crumbs outside the white kitchen tent. Standing at the counter, I buttered bread for the sandwiches I was making for the crew. I slathered peanut butter on, scraping the jar clean. *It's a good thing we're heading out today,* I thought. *There's not much food left.* Ten days ago we'd packed in to set up camps at Danaher and Cooney. Because the forest fire had consumed Cooney Creek Camp, we'd worked night and day to rebuild it. All the hard work made us hungry, and we sure put a hurt on our stock of food. The last cans of stew simmered in a pot on the woodstove.

I stuffed sandwiches into plastic sandwich bags. I was worried. *How are we going to get out of here? No matter which way we go, everything's on fire.* We didn't have any way to contact the outside world for information on the hotspots. I pondered the routes. North would take us days to get to some green areas. *But I don't want to be in the green. That means there's fuel for the fire.* South was the most direct route to the ranch, but we knew it would be dangerous to ride through the deep canyon covered with ash. Even with the river rushing below, we could get trapped if the fire hit. East...we didn't know what was happening over there. Because of the mountainous terrain, we couldn't see far in that direction. West would take four days, and we didn't know what the fire was doing over there either. I screwed the red lid on the empty peanut butter jar. *Which way will have the least amount of fire to go through? Lord, please show us which way to go.*

Pushing open the tent flap, I stepped outside and looked up the burned canyon behind camp. Fresh snow had fallen this morning, but the heat from the smoldering ground had melted it in places. Charred logs continued to fizzle and steam. Smoke belched from the pits created when the fire spread through the duff. I walked around our campfire, peering up the trail. The ash that had covered the ground a foot deep when we rode in had become a gooey mess. Although the snow had knocked down some of the flames, the forest fire was a long way from going out.

I squinted, hoping to see the guys with the horses and mules. When we'd arrived, we'd unbuckled the halters and shoed the critters out of camp just like we always did. They headed up the mountain to graze on what was left of the green grass. We'd kept a couple horses in camp to use when needed and so we could wrangle the herd in when it was time to leave.

This morning Allen and Jeff slipped on their cowboy hats, saddled their horses, and rode up the mountain to find the herd. After searching the hillsides and the high mountain meadows, they'd returned without them. Because of the fire, the animals had obviously moved beyond their normal grazing area to find enough food. The cowboys left again, this time recruiting the boss, Bill, to track the herd through the high-country rockslides. They'd left hours ago. I walked a bit farther and stared up the trail. I was antsy to get going. If we took the shortest route, it was a little more than a four hour ride to the trailhead—and that was on a good day. We'd be slogging through wet ash and skirting hotspots this time. *Who knows which way we'll go out or how long it will take.*

A cold breeze blew down the canyon and into camp, carrying the putrid smell of the wet and charred trees and brush. *Yuck. It'll be so nice to breathe fresh air again.* I turned to go back into the cook tent. The sound of hooves clicking against rocks on the trail caught my attention. I looked around and the herd of horses and mules came around the corner. They swished their tails and playfully tossed their heads as they strolled into the newly built charred-rail corral. The guys tied their horses to the hitching rack. I hollered, "Lunch is on. Come and get it."

In minutes we were sitting around the campfire spooning down stew and sipping strong coffee. We looked like we'd been playing in a coal bin. Everything we'd handled the last few days had been burned and converted to charcoal. Our faces, hands, and clothes were smudged black. I dipped my spoon into the bowl and watched Bill as he chewed on his dark moustache. I knew he was figuring out which direction to ride today.

Suddenly the horses whinnied and the mules brayed. We all looked down the trail. A few hundred yards away, out of the blackened forest, appeared a man riding a sorrel mule. He was wearing a long, yellow slicker and a silver hardhat. Puzzled, we looked at each other and then watched him dodge around pits of flames. His hardhat was tipped down over his eyes; the collar of the yellow slicker was turned up. He didn't say a thing. He just rode straight toward us. Cradling my steaming coffee cup in my hands, I took a sip. *He looks like he works for the Forest Service. What's he doing back here?*

When he got within 10 feet, he broke into a grin and swept off the hardhat revealing his white hair. "Is it ever great to see you guys!" It was Jack, the owner of the outfit! We hadn't seen him since we'd split up a few days ago. He'd ridden home to see if the people and ranch had survived the fire.

Jack stepped out of the saddle. We surrounded him, peppering him with questions. "How is everybody? Is the ranch still standing? How far did the fire run?"

Jack held up his hand. "Remember the night we watched the fire blow up from the Danaher Valley? That's when the people at the ranch were told to evacuate." Jack's grin faded, his eyes looked pained as he relayed the story. The folks at the ranch scurried to pack a few things and moved them onto Kleinschmidt Flats, a meadow a few miles away.

Jack's fingers rubbed the edge of the metal hat as he told about how the hot wind howled and blasted down the canyon toward the home place. It was dark outside except for the glow of the fire and the red embers the wind was swirling and raining down. Terrified, the ranch crew had stood in the meadow praying. The blaze thundered and roared, flames and smoke filling the sky. Then, like a bomb, the 200- to 300-foot wall of flames exploded down the canyon. *Wa-whoosh!* It headed straight for the ranch, incinerating everything in its path. Just as abruptly, the wind changed. At the last possible moment, the wall of flames turned 90 degrees, sweeping due east. The inferno never paused as it rolled on.

The sorrel mule rubbed its head on Jack's arm. Jack lightly tugged the reins, asking him to back up. "The fires are still raging. The Forest Service has thousands of firefighters digging fire lines. Helicopters are dumping retardant and water on the flames. National Guard troops have been called in to help." Jack drew in a deep breath and lowered his voice. "The Forest Service has closed the wilderness. I came out here to help you get out. I was afraid you'd go to the east, and the fires are still exploding over there. I don't know if anybody could make it through." Jack slipped on the hat. "The worst part was the blockade the Forest Service set up on the road to the trailhead. They wouldn't let me ride in to get you. They said it was too dangerous." Jack shrugged. "Maybe they didn't believe you were still alive." A grin lit up his face. "I knew if I looked official I could get past that barricade. One of the fire-crew guys at the ranch loaned me the hat." He tapped the hardhat.

"And this." He tugged on the yellow slicker and chuckled. "I loaded my mule into the stock rack on the pickup and drove to the blockade. They waved me through."

I frowned, my mind wrestling to grasp the situation. *What if the guys had found the horses right away, and we'd left first thing this morning? And perhaps gone east?* I sipped my coffee and looked at Jack. *He could have chosen not to come when the Forest Service announced the wilderness closed. And he could have turned back when he was stopped at the barricade and told it was too dangerous. But we were his crew and his family. We were his responsibility, and he acted on what he knew was the right thing to do. If he wouldn't have come in, we might have headed east and...*

I stopped my panicked thoughts and turned to God in prayer.

> *Lord, thank You for putting people in my life who love me and follow You. Give me the courage to do what's right, no matter what the cost. Amen.*

50

Peace in the Storm

Only God gives inward peace, and I depend on him.
PSALM 62:5 CEV

Clouds hung over the smoldering mountains as the sun slipped down to be even with the top of the ridge. I sat relaxed as Britt moseyed down the trail. Behind me three guys pulled strings of mules. The deep, mucky ash on the trail slurped each time the animals lifted their hooves. I glanced at the charred, skeletal trees that lined the mountains as far as I could see. The summer forest fire had done its destructive work. The bit of snow last night had soaked the ash, but it wasn't enough to put out the fire. It had tamed it quite a bit though.

Last week, when the fire unexpectedly became a raging inferno, we'd been setting up hunting camps. We'd been surrounded by flames ever since. Today we were riding through the charred remains of the forest to get home.

God, my bones ache from all the work rebuilding camp—the cutting and hauling logs, setting up the tents, straightening nails, cooking, and all the other little jobs. I coughed a deep raspy cough. *I'm so tired of the flames, Lord. Especially the black, dense smoke and acrid smell. And the animals that were killed or lost their moms…my heart aches.*

I was emotionally overloaded from living between walls of flames. I wanted out…now. I reached down and stroked Britt's neck. Fires that were still scattered across the hillsides crackled and popped occasionally. Charred logs fizzled and hissed from the dampness, trying to once again erupt into flames. The bitter smell of smoke choked the air. Not a sound of any living thing could be heard…except the squish of hooves and rubbing of leather as we moved down the trail. I didn't see a squirrel or hear a bird chirping or cawing. Some of the wildlife had moved out of the area as the flames approached. Some had been killed by the fire.

Grief hit me hard. I slumped in the saddle. Only a short while ago the forest I'd ridden through had consisted of green lodgepole pines, streams lined with wildflowers, and meadows of knee-deep, green grass that rustled in the breeze. Now the pines were black spikes and a gray mass covered the ground. *Everything's gone…fried to a crisp.*

The trail narrowed to only a few feet wide and skirted a scarred hillside. I groaned as Britt rounded a bend. Blocking the trail were a dozen trees that had fallen on top of each other. I moaned. *I'm exhausted. I don't want to cut out another tree.* We'd discovered that the fire had done a strange thing—burning the *inside* of the pines, through the channels of sap, going all the way down through the roots, severing the trees' hold on the earth. For the past five hours we'd been sawing downed trees—necessary just to get through. In some spots it took us hours to travel a mile because there were hundreds of charred pines clogging the path. It wouldn't be so bad if we had a chainsaw, but they were illegal in the wilderness area. We were using a two-man crosscut saw.

I turned and hollered to the guys, "Get out the saw." I stepped out of the saddle and onto the trail. Holding Britt's reins, I watched Bill untie the eight-foot-long saw that was bent over the two packs on his lead mule. From the top of his cowboy hat to the bottom of his boots, he was covered with black soot, just like the rest of us. For the past week everything we touched had been charred: the logs we sat on while we ate around the campfire, the trees we tied our horses to, the rails we cut and built into new corrals and frames for some tents, and now the trees we cut and hauled off the trail. Our hands and gloves were covered in charcoal, and then we'd touch our faces to wipe off sweat, satisfy an itch, or readjust our clothes. Blackness soon covered every inch of us. We looked like coal miners. I glanced down at my now-black blue jeans. Even the bridle reins were covered with soot. *I'm so sick of black. And I stink like I've been standing in the middle of a bonfire. I want out of here!*

On the uphill side of the narrow trail, Bill shinnied past Britt. He was carrying the saw over his shoulder, and Jeff followed on his heels. Bill climbed over the tall pile of logs, and Jeff positioned himself opposite him. Each of them grabbed a wooden handle and set the saw on the top log. Bill pulled; then Jeff pulled; Bill pulled; Jeff pulled. Back and forth they went. Zip…zip…zip…zip. The teeth of the saw cut into the log. Gradually they increased the speed, and the metal saw sang as they settled into a steady rhythm: zing…zing…zing. With each pull, a small pile of sawdust fell to the ground. I sighed and closed my eyes. *This is going to take forever.*

The sun dipped behind the mountain, and twilight settled over the canyon. Bill and Jeff set down the saw. Chunks of logs littered the downhill side of the trail. Bill ran his hand through his hair, and sweat dripped through soot. He nodded at me. Jeff wiped the sweat off his chin and winced as he rubbed his upper arms. He walked over to Britt. I handed him the reins and climbed over the log pile.

Allen, who had been holding the lead ropes of the other horses and mules, shinnied his six-five frame along the narrow ledge, past the horses and mules, and positioned himself across from me. Simultaneously our gloved hands grasped the saw handles and set it on the log that was now on top. Slowly I pulled, and then Allen pulled. Zip…zip…zip. Every muscle in my arms screamed from all the cutting I'd done that day. Finally the saw sang as we hit our rhythm: zing…zing…zing. Sweat poured down my neck and trickled down my back. After a short while my arm muscles seized up. I lost the rhythm of the saw and didn't have the strength to start again. I nodded to Bill to replace me.

Taking Britt's reins I sat in the wet ashes on the hillside. *I wish we could stop and sleep, but we don't have enough food. And all the tents and sleeping bags are back at the hunting camp. Besides, with all the smoldering brush and falling trees, there isn't a safe spot to set up a tent.* I turned my thoughts to God. *When are we going to get out of here, Lord? I'm dog-tired, and I'm sure the guys are too.* I leaned forward, holding the lead rope in my hands. It was black, of course. So were my sleeves and the ground I sat on. I shook my head and glanced up at Britt. In the fading daylight his beautiful gold coat and striking ivory-colored mane and tail almost glowed. "With the exception of the little bit of char on your legs, Britt, you're about the only thing around here that isn't black." I smiled as the sound of the guys pulling the saw rang through the canyon.

With a glint in my eye I stood up. I dipped my glove into the ashes on the ground and walked next to my horse's shoulder. In front of the saddle I carefully drew a four-inch circle. My glove ran out of ash, so I dipped it again and finger-painted spokes radiating out from the circle. Chuckling, I stepped back and admired the sun I'd drawn. *He looks like an Indian pony! God, what do You think of my handiwork?* Moving to Britt's hip, I dipped my glove into the ash and drew a star. For the next 15 minutes I purposely disappeared from the torment of the fire by escaping to a beautiful place where I finger painted my horse with God.

The sound of the saw stopped. I looked up. Bill stood next to the last logs on the trail. He raised his dark eyebrows and asked, "Are you up to it?" I nodded. My arms still ached, but my mind was refreshed. The mini vacation far, far away, had been wonderful.

> *Lord, please remind me when the whole world around me is falling apart—even if it's burning up—that my spirit can disappear into a peaceful place with You for a much-needed reprieve. Amen.*

51

Wa-whoosh!

*Look deep into my heart, God, and find out
everything I am thinking. Don't let me follow evil ways,
but lead me in the way that time has proven true.*

PSALM 139:23-24 CEV

It has to be close to midnight. I looked at the thick, black clouds covering the sky and blocking the moonlight. Glowing embers and red flames from the forest fire flickered across our black faces and cast eerie shadows through the woods. Sweat dripped through the soot on Bill's face as his gloved hand pulled the crosscut saw. I stood opposite him, doing my part. Sweat rolled down my back as I pulled with both hands wrapped around the wooden handle. Slowly the saw dug into the log. Zip...zip...zip. The muscles in my arms screamed in pain from pulling the saw through what seemed like thousands of charred trees that had fallen across the trail. I closed my eyes. *Rebecca, don't be a wimp. You've got to pull faster. Make the saw sing.* I took a deep breath and summoned my fading energy. In my mind I quickened my pace, and I forced my arms to follow. Zing...zing...zing. A small pile of sawdust fell. Rhythmically we pulled the old-fashioned tool.

Steam rose from the charred logs that littered the ground. The remnants of the fire and the dampness from the earlier snowfall made them pop and hiss as moisture evaporated. The air was filled with a musty, moldy odor and a light haze of smoke. I coughed, the effort racking my body. My eyes burned, my lungs ached, and my throat was raw from breathing the acrid smoke for the last week.

Had it only been a week since this canyon was draped in colors that symbolized life: greens, golds, and reds? The inferno that had blasted through this canyon at more than 160 acres a minute incinerated everything in its path. The only things left behind were small, localized fires, charred remains of trees and bushes, drifts of ashes, orphaned and dead animals…and us.

We were making our way down the trail toward home, interrupted at almost every turn it seemed by fallen trees that blocked the way. We'd been taking turns all day at the saw. Bill and I being spelled by Allen and Jeff when we were too tired to go on. We were still miles from the trailhead.

A breeze whistled through the canyon. Suddenly we heard the crack of a burned tree snapping off, followed by a rumbling crash. The falling tree had snapped another tree, which had snapped another tree, causing a chain reaction. An entire stand of trees thundered to the ground. A chill ran down my spine as I stared at Bill. The tree roots had been burned, making all the trees unstable. I pulled the crosscut saw while staring suspiciously at the trees towering around us.

A drop of sweat rolled into my eye. It stung. While pulling the saw blade toward me, I brushed my eye with my sleeve. I lost the rhythm, and instead of pulling, I pushed. The saw bound up, bunching in the middle until it was pinched to a stop. I glanced at Bill. Sweat dripped off the corner of his dark moustache. "I'm sorry," I said as I frowned.

Slowly we started back up again. My arms throbbed. With each heartbeat, I could feel the blood pound through my body. I pulled and pulled. Zip…zip…zip. But before the saw started to sing, the muscles in my arms melted. My hand muscles quit working, and I dropped the saw handle. In the flickering firelight I looked at Bill. My heart ached as I admitted, "I'm done. I don't have the strength to pull anymore."

Bill nodded and yelled, "Allen, I need you to come and pull."

My shoulders drooped as I shuffled over to Britt. I sat in the ashes on the hillside by his shoulder. While I listened to the cadence of the saw, accusations chanted through my mind: *You're letting the crew down. You aren't pulling your weight.* My body hacked and trembled as I coughed.

I looked through the corpselike trees. Many still had tiny flames lapping at them. Deep pits in the duff-covered ground spouted flames that periodically licked the sky. Everywhere around me were death and destruction. *This is about as close to hell as a person can get while living,* I decided. The fire in the pit closest to me snapped to life, tossing glowing embers into the sky. The fire smoldering in the decaying pine needles and other dead plant matter gradually dried out the earth, making it crumble into the pit. *How many of these pits are smoldering underground, weakening the earth above them?* This was an unseen menace I hadn't considered before. I shuddered.

When the guys finished cutting this pile of charred logs, they tied the crosscut saw back on the mule. We stepped into our saddles, and I urged Britt forward. Slouching from exhaustion, I rested my hands on the saddle horn and coughed. Muffled hoofbeats squished through the wet ash behind me. Catching the rhythm, memories of words spoken to me in anger echoed: *You quitter! You're just a sissy girl. Now you've done it! Weakling.* I slid deeper in the saddle. I was too tired and weak to resist the devil's arrows being shot straight into my heart.

The trail funneled us onto a narrow, rocky ledge above the North Fork River. As the river rushed over boulders a long way below, trees continued to spew flames on both sides of the trail. As Britt plodded forward, his hooves clicked on the rocks. Just as I noticed that the sound had changed, the earth crumbled underneath us. I grabbed Britt's mane as we dropped four feet straight down, ending up in a fire pit. As the earth opened up, oxygen rushed in. *Wa-whoosh!* The fire roared and vomited flames. They engulfed us, shooting taller than my head. Rearing up, Britt leaped out of the flames and onto the trail. He tossed his head, his muscles bunched as he launched down the trail. I quickly but gently pulled the reins. Britt reared again as fear told him to take flight. I allowed him to go forward a few steps and then pulled him to a stop. I checked for any flames or smoldering embers on Britt's coat and my clothes.

I turned in my saddle to look at Bill. About six feet of trail had disappeared. The fire pit belched flames, eerily silhouetting him. His horse tossed its head, its eyes wide, nostrils flaring. Gathering the reins, Bill urged it to the edge of the pit. He leaned forward and abruptly dug his heels into the horse's side. It gathered itself and leaped through the flames. Landing on the trail, Bill walked his horse forward. One by one his string of mules followed. Allen and his string of mules were next, followed by Jeff and his group.

Adrenaline was pulsing through Britt and me. As we moved forward I kept a tight rein to keep him from taking off. I could feel his muscles bunching as he gathered himself to run. I reined him in and stopped. He tipped his weight back like he was going to rear again. I nudged him forward. He took a couple steps, bobbed his head, and then stretched his legs into a mile-eating walk.

The river roared beneath us as the ledge skirted the folds of the mountain. Fire pits on sidehills haphazardly burst into flames. Gradually Britt's head lowered as he settled down. I took a deep, cleansing breath. Suddenly the earth crumbled beneath us again. Flames engulfed us as Britt reared on his haunches and leaped out of another pit. I felt his muscles tense, and he tucked his head to buck. He wanted to take control and run. I held my breath and yanked his head up and around, so he would look straight down and see how far it was and know he needed to be careful. He bounced on stiff front legs several more times before stopping and snorting. Breathing a sigh of relief, I turned just as Bill's horse sailed over the flaming pit, followed by his mules and the rest of our group.

My legs quivered in the stirrups as I nudged Britt into a walk. The firelight cast shifting shadows on either side of the ledge. We rounded the bend. Charred logs, stacked 10 or so high, created a fence diagonally across the trail. My saddle creaked as I turned and hollered, "Bill, get the saw."

As Bill shinnied along the hill with the saw over his shoulder, he looked at me questioningly. Slumped next to Britt, I sadly shook my head no. I still couldn't drum up the strength to help. Instantly arrows of condemnation pierced my heart again. *What a loser. You weakling. They'd be better off with someone else on their crew.* I sighed and sat in the ashes on the steep bank. Glancing downhill I watched the "lid" of a fire pit collapse. Flames and sparks shot into the air. I shivered. *There's no warning before they collapse. We're at their mercy.*

The rhythmic sound of the saw zipped through the night. A nearby pit spewed flames. *Almost like these thoughts of mine.* I took a deep breath. *Nobody's spoken those hateful words to me in years. Where did they come from?* I must have stuffed them into my heart, and just like the fire that burned underground, they churned inside, eroding my core without me realizing it. They'd insidiously smoldered until my barriers were weak and they could erupt into my consciousness.

But, God, I don't understand. Why do they still have power over me? Instantly I knew the answer. When the words had been spoken with venomous anger, I'd been hurt because I was afraid they were true. Instead of opening them up and comparing them to the truth of God's Word, I had tucked them away intact and powerful. And the devil had used today's situation to unlock the arsenal and launch the deadly arrows.

Then God spoke to my spirit, "You can allow those arrows to pierce your heart or you can use the shield of My Word to stop them."

Zip...zip...zip. The saw sound drifted through the woods. For the next half hour I pulled one "angry words" arrow after another out of my heart, remembering who had uttered them and consciously choosing to forgive. Then I incinerated the memory and pain using the truth of God's Word. *I'm not a wimp. I haven't used a crosscut saw enough to develop strong arm muscles. And I have less muscle mass than the guys. I am a female; God chose to create me into a girl.*

The rest of the trip was filled with fire pits to survive and logs to cut. After falling in a few more times, Britt's terror made him unsafe to ride. I rounded up my willpower and energy and walked the last seven miles to the trailhead.

> *Lord, when I'm exhausted and the devil is shooting arrows at me, remind me to hold up my shield of faith in You. Amen.*

52

Deserted

The LORD is with you when you are with him.
If you seek him, he will be found by you.

2 CHRONICLES 15:2

Thick clouds cloaked the sky. It was after midnight, but I didn't need a flashlight. Holding the reins, I shuffled down the trail leading Britt. Hoofbeats echoed through the woods from the horses and mules the crew behind me were in charge of. We were riding through the burning wilderness area, on our way home after setting up two hunting camps. Already we'd encountered hundreds of downed trees on the trail we'd had to cut through and fire pits that collapsed the ground below us. I was leading Britt because he was too nervous to be ridden.

Both sides of the canyon along this stretch had been burned black and were draped with spot fires. The light from them flickered, eerily illuminating the trail. I was so exhausted I could barely slide one boot in front of the other. I glanced at the next curve in the trail. *Only minutes to the trailhead, the pickup, and the ranch. I can't wait to get out of the fire, take a shower to get this soot and bonfire smell off me, crawl between clean sheets, and drift off to sleep in a safe place.*

The hillsides of the canyon steamed, filling the air with stinky smoke from all around us. My eyes burned and my lungs ached. I coughed. Piles of charred logs littered the ground. Small flames still burned hot, making them fizzle and pop. Last night we'd gotten a skiff of snow that had calmed the fire a bit.

Suddenly a tree snapped. I winced and braced myself, quickly glancing to my side to see where it was going to fall. *Crack!* It smashed into the burned trees on my left. The stand of trees tumbled into each other, falling like dominoes. They hit the ground. *Thwack!* Britt jumped forward, smacking into me. I tottered sideways, caught myself, and held on tight as Britt hit the end of the reins. He stopped, all four legs spread apart for stability but ready to run again. He snorted. With flared nostrils he stared at the heap of burned trees that had fallen into a pile next to the trail. I stepped next to him and stroked his neck. "We're almost home, buddy. Hang in there." At my voice, he lowered his head and put it next to my chest, almost as if he wanted to hide.

I continued down the trail, leading him. My head hung down and my arms were limp by my side. I loosely held the reins. I was emotionally and physically exhausted from being surrounded by flames. Even my mind had drifted into a haze. With my last ounces of strength I lifted my legs to swing them forward, trying to use the beat of hooves to help me keep moving. *You can make it, Rebecca. Around the next bend is the trailhead. And Jack said he'd leave a truck for us.* In what seemed a lifetime ago but was only this morning, Jack had ridden into camp to let us know how to get out of the forest fire. The wilderness had been closed and the roads to the trailheads blockaded because of the intensity of the fire. To get through the Forest Service roadblocks, he'd dressed in firefighter clothes. There was only one way we could ride out through the fire-affected forest, and he'd risked his life to come tell us. His parting words as he turned his mule to leave were "I'll make sure there's a pickup at the trailhead for you." Then he hightailed it back to the ranch. We followed as soon as we'd packed the gear on the mules.

I watched a fire pit explode, spitting embers into the night sky. My mouth was sticky from breathing the dry, sooty air. *I am so done with this. Only a quarter of a mile, and we'll be at the corrals, the pickup, and then home.* The idea of stepping into a truck sounded soooo good. I swung my legs faster. The trail turned downhill. With each step, the muscles in my legs screamed. Finally I turned down the last bit of trail to the corrals. As soon as they came into sight I glanced around. No pickup. Even the tack-shed trailer had been pulled out. The place was deserted. Only charred earth and spot fires filled the little meadow. I stopped, slumped, and groaned. Behind me, one by one, I heard the guys come to a halt and moan.

Bill nudged his horse next to me and looked down. "Looks like the fire went through so they had to evacuate." In the firelight, he took a deep breath. "I'll lead. I know a way we can cut cross-county to save time and energy. It's only six miles to the ranch." He turned his horse. Slowly I gimped down the trail. *Only six more miles. We might as well be going to the moon. I'm done in.*

Mile after mile my boots ground down the gravel road. Gradually the spot fires became farther apart. We reached a grassy flat without any fires. The clouds still covered the moon, so we were plunged into darkness. I blindly scuffled along. I stubbed my toe in a pothole and nearly collapsed. Britt patiently nuzzled me, encouraging me forward. I reached back and rubbed his forehead and mumbled, "Are you feeling better?" He leaned into my hand. I separated the reins, looping them on each side of his neck, stepped into the stirrup, and managed to heave myself up. I melted into the saddle as Britt lengthened his stride to catch up with the pack strings.

Bill reined his horse off the dirt road and into a grassy field that followed the base of the mountain. For the next hour we opened and closed barbed-wire gates as we wound through fields. Finally we reached the ranch and rode straight into the barn. When Bill flipped the switch to the floodlights, we gasped. The barn was empty...deserted. Not one saddle hung on the rack, not one bridle hung on a peg, not one animal remained. Everything had been evacuated.

What had Jack said? I thought back to his visit. *He'd said they'd only grabbed a few things and moved them to the Flats and that the firestorm had blown past the ranch.* I'd assumed they would be moving things back in and getting ready for hunting season. In frustration I clenched my teeth. *I know Jack said, "See you at the ranch tonight."* I groaned.

The guys and I looked at each other in shock, and then we got to work. We stripped the saddles off of the stock, led them to the pasture, and turned them loose.

Flipping off the lights in the barn, we walked through the darkness to the lodge. Visions of a hot meal, shower, and clean sheets raced through my head. But when the screen door squeaked open and we turned on the lights, those thoughts were crushed. Our footsteps echoed through the hallway into the kitchen. The table and chairs were gone. We looked at each other, and the guys spread out in different directions to see if anything was left. I walked into the bathroom to wash the soot off my face, arms, and hands, but the towels were gone. There wasn't even a bar of soap! Walking back to the kitchen, I opened a cupboard. Not a plate, a glass, or a crumb of food was to be found. Frantically I rummaged through the drawers. Not a spoon or a pot. Disgustedly I slumped against the counter in the kitchen as the guys came back and reported no beds, sheets, or pillows. Not a couch, a chair, or even a rug. I checked the driveway. Not even a vehicle in the driveway so we could drive to Kleinschmidt Flats. Briefly I closed my eyes. Hollowness drifted through my soul. *After all we've been through, now we've been deserted.*

Huddled in the kitchen, we looked to Bill for direction. He took off his hat and set it on the counter. "Let's get some sleep. We'll get things squared around in the morning." The boys ambled into the lodge great room, curled up on the floor by the fireplace, and fell asleep. I got up and stumbled into the dining room and crumpled onto the bare floor. I lay on my side, using my arm for a pillow. My body ached. I smelled like I'd been in a smoker all week. Staring into the darkness, my mind reeled with images of flames, the horror of falling into fire pits, and the hours sawing through logs. All I'd wanted today was to get home, take a shower, and safely snuggle between clean sheets. But home had disappeared. The ranch was like a ghost town. When I closed my eyes, a still small voice nudged my spirit: "But I haven't deserted you." A warm feeling flowed through me as I drifted off to sleep.

God, thank You for reminding me that my home is with You and that You are always with me. When I feel alone, please remind me that I'm alone because I left You, not the other way around. Amen.

Epilogue on the Fire

The next day we found out what had happened. When Jack left the camp and rode back to the trailhead and ranch, the fire had sprung to life again. He couldn't leave a truck at the corrals because the heat would have ignited the gas.

The crew at the ranch had been told to evacuate, so they'd packed up everything they could—the gear, equipment, horses, household furnishings. They were operating on the belief that if the fire got that far, it would destroy everything left. Exhausted from the emotional toll of the fire's threat and from packing up the entire ranch in two days, they'd set up camp on Kleinschmidt Flats. Since we were so late because of the trees we'd had to cut, they didn't know when we'd arrive. They figured we'd arrive during daylight and join them there. They didn't know how tired and hungry and exhausted we would be.

Thousands of firefighters had been recruited to dig fire lines. Helicopters had been based at the ranch and made multiple runs each day to douse the flames with retardant and water. The morning after we rode out of the wilderness, we discovered that 2,000 National Guard troops had been deployed, and they'd set up a tent village in one of our horse pastures a few miles away from the ranch house. By the time the fire was contained, it had burned more than 240,000 acres.

In spite of all the manpower that was brought in, nothing could stand against the ferocity of the raging inferno. Nothing except the prayers of the thousands of people who were threatened, had been evacuated, and around the nation who watched what was happening on the news. Within a week, God turned on the "fall rain faucet" and drenched the fire, although some of the fire pits burned until spring.

And the guests? The ranch called them to let them know the situation. When we knew the fire danger was over, we called them back... and they came anyway. Our preparations at Cooney Camp survived the remnants of the fire, so when the hunters arrived we packed them in and went about our work.

53

Riding Lead

*Yet our God gave us the courage to
declare his Good News to you boldly.*

1 Thessalonians 2:2 nlt

The wheeze of the respirator and the throb of the heart monitor cut the sticky air of the Intensive Care Unit hospital room. Tubes wound around Danny like a hangman's noose. *How can this be?* I wondered. *Danny's only in his early thirties.* I fluffed his pillow and pushed back the dark hair on his forehead. "I'll stop by tomorrow," I said as I gently squeezed his hand.

A single tear rolled down Danny's face as he gritted his teeth, the clear respirator tube getting in the way. He nodded his head and weakly squeezed back.

I poked my head into the waiting room where the pastor sat. "Have you had a chance to talk to him about the Lord?"

He nodded.

"Did he pray the prayer?" I asked.

He shook his head.

I shuffled out of the building, got into my car, and slammed the door. *What is wrong with me? Why didn't I say something to Danny about Jesus?*

I drummed my fingers on the steering wheel as I pulled out on the street. A month ago Danny was riding horses, rounding up cattle, and helping his neighbors with their branding. A strapping cowboy, Danny and I had worked with wild horses together the year before. This spring he'd been diagnosed with Hodgkin's disease (also called Hodgkin's lymphoma). He'd been rushed through chemotherapy. A couple of days ago his lungs filled with fluid, so the doctors had pumped them out and put him on a respirator.

I drove to the barn, saddled Czar, and mentally beat myself up as I rode down the trail. *Danny's heard it all before,* I rationalized. I kicked Czar into a trot. I pictured myself standing in Danny's room. "Danny, what do you think about God?" In my mind I could see him laughing. He loved the rough-and-tough cowboy life. He didn't have the time or need for "weak, sissy, God stuff."

I slowed Czar to a walk as I thought about the situation. He's in ICU. *His situation must be pretty serious if they've put him on a respirator.* My guts tied in knots. As a Christian, I have good news I could have shared...the saving grace and love of Jesus. *But what would Danny say if I brought it up?* I knew I needed to tell him, but I was afraid of his ridicule.

The next afternoon Danny showed improvement. When I got there the respirator was gone. Danny croaked a hello, his throat still raw from the tube. I smiled. *He's improving; I can wait.* Then Danny coughed... a hoarse cough that ravaged his weak body. He brushed a tear from his eye. I glanced over his bony hand, his pale face, and his sunken eyes. *What if he doesn't pull through?*

I pulled a chair next to his bed and twisted a strand of my hair. *Better get to it or I'll lose my nerve.* I took a deep breath and spoke. "Danny, there's something I've been wanting to share with you."

His voice graveled, he asked, "What's that?"

"I don't know how to..."

He raised a bushy eyebrow.

I blurted, "Have you ever heard anything about Jesus?"

He leaned back in bed and then sat up as another deep, raspy cough shook his body. He wheezed when he replied, "A lot of folks have told me about Him."

"Did you accept him as your Savior?"

Danny shrugged his shoulders and sank back into the bed.

"Has anybody told you *how* to make Him your Savior?" I persisted. He shook his head.

I was shocked. For weeks friends, family, and pastors had been praying and visiting with Danny, waiting for him to accept Jesus...but no one had remembered to tell him how to go about doing it.

"Would you like to accept Him as your Savior?" I asked.

Danny brushed his fingers through his hair as he whispered, "I'm scared. Scared I won't make it out of here. Yeah."

I wrapped my fingers around Danny's skeletal hand. "It's easy. All you have to do is talk to God. I'll help you. Repeat this prayer after me." As I spoke, Danny's voice echoed my words:

> "Lord, I am a sinner and can't save myself. I believe that Jesus Christ died on the cross for my sins. He rose from the dead three days later so I can have eternal life and live with Him forever. I'm asking You, Lord Jesus, to come into my heart to be my Savior, to live in me, and to guide me from this day forward. Amen."

Tears streamed down Danny's face as he shook from a silent sob. I handed him a Kleenex and took one myself. After a moment he breathed a deep, contented sigh. He wiped his eyes and asked, "What's heaven like?"

"I don't know exactly. I hope the beauty of earth is a reflection of heaven—the mountains and valleys."

Danny settled back into the pillows. "Do you think there are horses and cows?"

I chuckled. "I sure hope so. If there are, when I get there I'll even let you ride lead on the herd. I'll ride drag and eat dust."

Danny smiled and weakly reached to shake my hand. "Deal."

Those were the last moments I shared with Danny. I went out of town on business, and when I came home, the phone was ringing. Danny's brother broke the news, saying, "Danny's gone."

Tears streamed down my face as I hung up. *What if I hadn't asked the question? What if I'd waited?*

I reached for a tissue and glanced at a picture hanging on my wall. A cowboy was herding horses across a creek, and the sun was glinting off the splashing water. I grinned. *Danny, I bet you're riding lead right now. You're one blessed cowboy.*

> *Lord, teach me to be courageous and bold enough to share Your good news with folks—even if I think they don't want to hear it. Amen.*

54

Saddle Up

If these devotions have piqued your curiosity about a relationship with Jesus Christ, I want you to know He loves and cares for you as much as He does me. And He wants you to be part of His forever family. Being a Christian isn't about going to church or being religious. It's about having a personal relationship with Jesus Christ. If you haven't accepted Jesus Christ as the Lord of your life or if you've gone astray from a previous commitment, I invite you to come to Christ today.

The first step is to realize you are a sinner. We *all* are sinners. Romans 3:23 says, "All have sinned and fall short of the glory of God." The next step is talking to Jesus. According to Romans 10:9, "If you confess with your mouth, 'Jesus is Lord,' and believe in your heart that God raised him from the dead, you will be saved." Jesus died on the cross and was raised from the dead as payment for your sin. It's time to ask Jesus to forgive your sins—past, present, and future—and to ask Him into your heart as your Lord and Savior:

> *God, I am a sinner and can't save myself. I believe that Your*
> *Son, Jesus Christ, died on the cross for my sins. He rose from*

the dead three days later so I can have eternal life and live
with You forever. I'm asking You, Jesus, to come into my heart
and be my Savior. Live in me and guide me from this day
forward. Thank You. Amen.

Welcome to the family! Now it's important to publicly express those beliefs and be baptized. Each day invest time with God by reading His Word, the Bible. And remember to saddle up with other Christians to ride the trail of life.

May you be blessed with an awesome adventure on God's trail.

With Christ's love,

Rebecca

Glossary

Little Girl modeling gear

1. Breast collar
2. Cinch
3. D-ring on packsaddle (front and back) used for sling rope
4. Halter
5. Lead rope
6. Packsaddle to tie loads onto animals
7. Mane (roached)
8. Saddlepad
9. Sling rope used to secure a load to a packsaddle

Barrel woodstove: A woodstove made out of a metal barrel.

Bay: A horse or mule with a deep, reddish-brown coat and a black mane and tail.

Breakaway: A circular piece of rope attached to a packsaddle and used to tie the pack animals together, one after another. When an emergency arises and the rope is pulled hard, it's supposed to come undone or "break," freeing the animal.

Breast collar: A strap that buckles on the left side of the saddle, runs across the critter's chest, and buckles on the right side. It prevents the saddle from slipping back when the animal is traveling uphill.

Bridle: The headgear put on a horse or mule to provide control. The "head-stall" part has an opening that goes behind and in front of the ears, with straps going down the sides of the animal's face to hold a bit (metal bar) in place in a horse's mouth. The bit rides behind the animal's teeth, so it is not uncomfortable. The reins are attached to the bit. When the reins are pulled back, the chin strap applies slight pressure to a nerve, getting the horse's attention.

Buck: When a horse has a tantrum, he jumps up and down, back and forth, and any which way in abrupt motions to toss the rider off his back. Sometimes horses kick up their heels in good-natured fun.

Cinch: A strap attached to the saddle on one side that is passed under the critter's belly and tied to the other side to hold the saddle or packsaddle tight to the animal's back.

Colt: A horse less than a year old. In general terms it refers to males or females, but specifically it means a young male horse.

Coleman gas lantern: A lantern that runs on white gas fuel.

D-ring: A metal, D-shaped ring. On packsaddles it's used to tie on the ropes that hold the load in place.

Duffel: A small bag with handles for packing clothing and personal items.

Duffel bag: A large bag for packing a sleeping bag and duffel together.

Elmer Fudd hat: Wool hat with a bill. Ear flaps are folded up inside. (See photo of Wind Dancer.)

Filly: A female horse under a year old.

Foal: A male or female horse under a year old.

Gelding: A male horse that has been neutered.

Green broke: A horse that has received very basic training.

Halter: Headgear for guiding a horse. Made of leather, nylon webbing, or rope, it's used to control an animal when leading him or to tie him up so he stays within a particular area.

Hitching rail: Two posts driven into the ground with a horizontal post about waist high connecting them. A permanent tie-up place for holding critters in one place while brushing or saddling and when you want them nearby for later use.

Hobble: A wide leather strap that buckles together around a horse or mule's ankle. A picket rope is tied to it and a picket pin driven into the ground so the animal can move within a specific area to eat, drink, and rest. *Hobbles* are two leather straps that buckle around a horse or mule's front ankles and are connected with approximately seven inches of chain or strap. Hobbles are used to control how fast and how far the critter can go. The animal can move about, just in small steps.

Kindling: Logs that have been split into thin lengths; used for starting campfires.

Lariat (also riata): A long, heavy-duty, braided rope. Used to catch horses and cows. Skilled people hold one end and create a loop on the other, which they throw 10 or more feet so it settles around the neck or feet of an animal.

Lead rope: A rope that attaches to a halter that is used for leading or tying up the animal.

Load: Whatever the critter is carrying on its packsaddle.

Mantie: Wrapping gear inside a heavy weight, white canvas tarp to create a compact load suitable for putting on a packsaddle.

Mare: A female horse.

Mule: A hybrid animal resulting from the breeding of a mare and a male donkey. Most mules are sterile, although there have been rare cases of female mules reproducing when mated with horses or donkeys.

Pack: Gear wrapped in a mantie tarp that will be loaded onto a packsaddle.

Packers: People who pack loads and tie them on to the packsaddles of mules.

Packsaddle: Specially designed saddle used for hauling equipment or supplies via an animal.

Pack string: Pack animals that have been tied together in single file.

Palomino: A horse with a gold coat, although the color isn't always vibrant. The mane and tail are usually ivory or white.

Picketing: After placing a "picket pin" (a stake driven into the ground), one end of a "picket rope" (a rope ranging from 10 to 40 feet in length) is tied to the pin and the other is attached to a hobble placed on one of the front ankles of a horse or mule. This allows the animal to forage but limits its roaming range.

Pulling string: Leading pack animals that are tied together down the trail.

Rear: When a horse stands on its hind legs only.

Roached: A closely shaved mane.

Rope corral: Ropes strung between trees about waist high to form temporary pens to hold critters within a certain area.

Sack out: Training a horse to not get frightened by objects and noises by lightly flapping material around him and against his body.

Saddlebags: Two leather pockets or bags attached together that tie onto the back of a saddle with one bag on each side of the horse. Used for carrying small supplies and food.

Saddle pad: A blanket slightly bigger than a saddle, often with foam inside, placed under a saddle to provide cushioning for the animal. This makes the saddle more comfortable for the horse by eliminating chafing ("saddle sores").

Slash pile: A pile of branches, vegetation, and other unwanted forest debris ready to be disposed of by burning.

Slicker: A raincoat.

Sling rope: A rope used to secure a load to a packsaddle. Applied properly, the sling rope enables a load to move just enough to make it comfortable for the pack animal.

Snubbin' post: A post solidly planted in the middle of a corral and used to tie horses to when gentling (taming) them or training them.

Sorrel: A horse or mule with fur that is chestnut or light reddish-brown in color.

Stampede strap: A strap used to hold a hat to a person's head. It can be attached by inserting both ends through holes on opposite sides of the hat, creating loops on each end and placing them around the crown. Another method is to use cotter pins to attach each end to the lining. The strap hangs below the chin and usually has a slider for adjusting length.

String: Slang for a pack string of critters.

White canvas wall tent: Large tents made of heavy-duty canvas bleached white.

Wickiup: A small tarp tied between trees that is used for minimal weather protection for sleeping outdoors without setting up a tent.

Wood cookstove: A cooking stove fueled by wood.

Wrangle: Moving horses, cows, and other herd animals in a specific direction and to a specific location.

Wrangler: A person who works with horses or mules on a ranch.

For more information about
Rebecca and her writing, go to
www.RebeccaOndov.com
or connect with her via Facebook.